PHILIPPINES
in Pictures

Colleen A. Sexton

T F
C B

Twenty-First Century Books

Contents

Website address: www.lernerbooks.com

Twenty-First Century Books
A division of Lerner Publishing Group
241 First Avenue North
Minneapolis, MN 55401 U.S.A.

Library of Congress Cataloging-in-Publication Data

Sexton, Colleen A., 1967–
    Philippines in pictures / by Colleen Sexton.
        p.   cm. — (Visual geography series)
    Includes bibliographical references and index.
    ISBN-13: 978-0-8225-2677-3 (lib. bdg. : alk. paper)
    ISBN-10: 0-8225-2677-8 (lib. bdg. : alk. paper)
    1. Philippines—Juvenile literature. I. Title. II. Series: Visual geography series (Minneapolis, Minn.)
DS655.S474 2006
959.9—dc22   2005017358

Manufactured in the United States of America
1 2 3 4 5 6 – BP – 11 10 09 08 07 06

INTRODUCTION

Made up of more than seven thousand islands, the Republic of the Philippines is an archipelago (group of islands) in the western Pacific Ocean. A geographically diverse nation, the Philippines contains large, modern cities, quiet rural villages, and remote island communities. The country is home to approximately 83 million people from more than eighty ethnic groups, giving the nation a rich cultural heritage. Most Filipinos trace their roots to the Asian mainland or to early island kingdoms located west of the Philippines. Malays—who came from the territories of present-day Indonesia and Malaysia—are the largest group to have established communities on the islands. These Malays and other immigrants form the many ethnic roots of the modern Filipino population.

For centuries the Philippines was a colony ruled by other nations. Its relationships with its former rulers—Spain and later the United States—live on in the religions, languages, and culture of the Philippines. Christian missionaries arrived in the sixteenth century as

part of a Spanish attempt to colonize the region. They brought the Spanish language as well as Christianity to the islands. The United States took over the archipelago in 1898 and introduced English. After the Philippines gained independence in 1946, more Filipinos began speaking the national language, which was later named Filipino.

Since 1946 the Filipinos have turned their attention to long-standing internal problems. High on this list of concerns is land distribution. For centuries huge parcels of land belonged to a small group of landowners. Poorly paid workers farmed these acreages. Since independence, Philippine governments have introduced land reform programs in order to redistribute territory to the nation's landless tenant farmers. Wealthy landowners, however, have hampered the reform efforts.

From 1965 to 1986, under the leadership of President Ferdinand Marcos, the Philippine economy suffered, and government corruption was widespread. For nine years of his presidency, Marcos imposed martial law in the Philippines, limiting the civil rights of Filipinos.

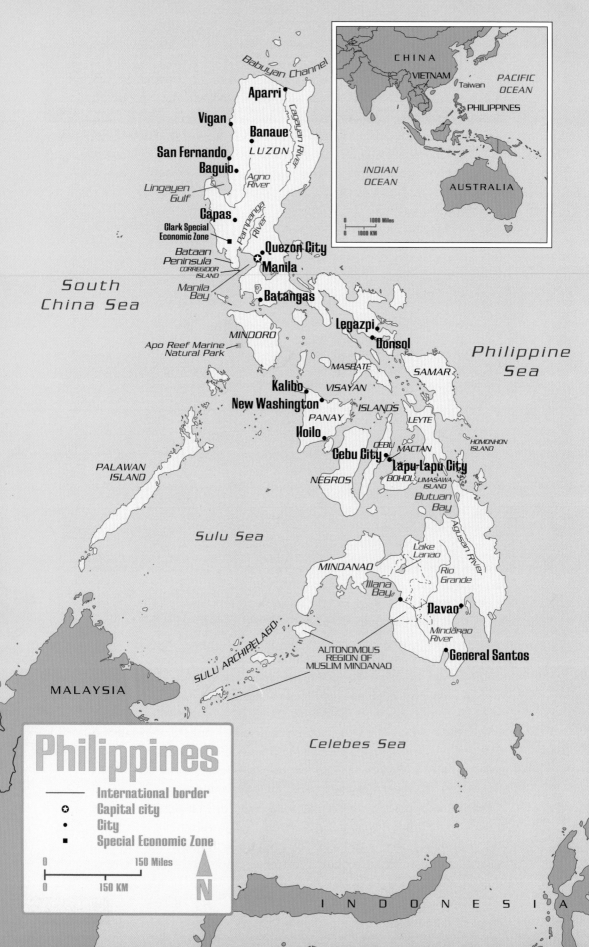

Bowing to pressure in 1986, he was forced out of office. Over the past two decades, the government has worked to restore democracy and to increase economic development.

President since 2001, Gloria Macapagal-Arroyo has boosted the economy by encouraging foreign investment in the Philippines. Despite economic growth, poverty plagues the country, particularly in rural areas. The government also faces threats from separatist groups and terrorist organizations. Arroyo has promised to fight terrorism and to stay focused on improving the way of life for all Filipinos.

THE LAND

The Philippine Islands lie at the western edge of the Pacific Ocean. To the north is the island of Taiwan. To the west, beyond the South China Sea, are Vietnam and China. The Philippines faces Malaysia and Indonesia across the Sulu and Celebes seas in the southwest. The portion of the Pacific Ocean on the eastern side of the archipelago is named the Philippine Sea.

Stretching across 1,100 miles (1,770 kilometers) of ocean, the Philippines contains more than 7,000 islands. Only about 150 of them, however, are bigger than 5 square miles (13 sq. km) in area. The nation's total land area is 115,830 square miles (300,000 sq. km), making it slightly larger than the state of Nevada.

◉ Topography

The territory of the Philippines may be divided into three main areas. Luzon (40,400 sq. mi or 104,600 sq. km), the largest island in the archipelago, anchors the northern end of the island chain. Mindanao

(36,500 sq. mi or 94,500 sq. km) ranks as the second-biggest landmass and sits at the archipelago's southern tip. Between these two pieces of territory lie islands that are known collectively as the Visayan Islands.

Not all Philippine territories fit into these three main regions. For example, west of the main body of the archipelago lies Palawan Island, a narrow strip of mountainous territory. Mindoro, an oval-shaped island between Palawan and Luzon, has a central mountain range and a wide coastal plain on its eastern side. The Sulu Archipelago sits southwest of Mindanao. A number of smaller islands also fall outside of the country's three principal geographical divisions.

Volcanic action and movements of the earth's crust formed the Philippine Islands, most of which are mountainous. About twenty of the country's peaks are active volcanoes. Long coastlines, which offer harbors for shipping and access to fishing waters, are also a main feature of the Philippines. The country has 22,549 miles (36,289 km) of coastline, more than twice the total length of the U.S. coastline.

LUZON Several mountain ranges run through Luzon, the archipelago's largest island. The Sierra Madre extends for more than 200 miles (320 km) along Luzon's northeastern coast and range from 3,500 to 5,000 feet (1,070 to 1,524 meters) in height. The rolling plain of the Cagayan Valley lies between the Sierra Madre and the Cordillera Central—the main range on Luzon. The Cordillera's peaks reach a height of 9,606 feet (2,928 m) at Mount Pulog.

ON THE RING OF FIRE

The Philippines lies on the Ring of Fire, a belt of volcanoes that circles the Pacific Ocean. Earthquakes often occur along the Ring of Fire, and the Philippines experiences an average of five per day. A major earthquake strikes the country about every ten years. In 1976 a powerful quake rocked Mindanao, killing eight thousand people. A 1990 earthquake on Luzon left countless buildings destroyed and one thousand people dead.

In central Luzon, the Cordillera range meets the Caraballo Mountains, which have an elevation of 2,000 to 5,000 feet (610 to 1,524 m). The flat central plain of the island extends westward from the Caraballos to the Zambales Mountains, a small chain that pushes south into the Bataan Peninsula. Manila Bay, the site of the nation's capital city of Manila, is a 770-square-mile (2,000 sq km) inlet of the South China Sea on Luzon's southwestern coast. Corregidor Island guards the inlet's mouth.

Several volcanoes dot Luzon. Located less than 100 miles (160 km) south of Manila, Mount Taal is a small but dangerous volcano that rumbles every few years. It has erupted numerous times since the sixteenth century.

An **earthquake-damaged building** in Luzon

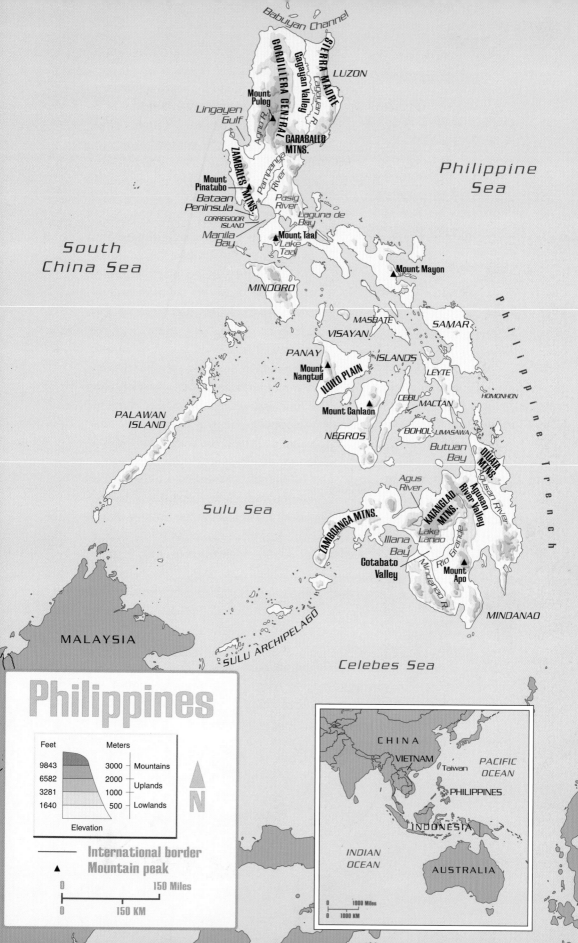

Babuyan Channel

CORDILLERA CENTRAL

SIERRA MADRE

Cagayan Valley

Cagayan R.

LUZON

Mount Pulog

Lingayen Gulf

Agno R.

CARABALLO MTNS.

ZAMBALES MTNS.

Pampanga River

Mount Pinatubo

Bataan Peninsula

Pasig River

Laguna de Bay

CORREGIDOR ISLAND

Manila Bay

Mount Taal

Lake Taal

Mount Mayon

MINDORO

MASBATE

VISAYAN

SAMAR

PANAY

Mount Nangtud

ILOILO PLAIN

ISLANDS

LEYTE

CEBU

MACTAN

HOMONHON

Mount Canlaon

NEGROS

BOHOL

LIMASAWA

Butuan Bay

DIUATA MTNS.

Agus River

Agusan River Valley

Agusan River

KATANGLAD MTNS.

ZAMBOANGA MTNS.

Illana Bay

Lake Lanao

Cotabato Valley

Mindanao R.

Rio Grande

Mount Apo

MINDANAO

South China Sea

Philippine Sea

Philippine Trench

Sulu Sea

PALAWAN ISLAND

MALAYSIA

SULU ARCHIPELAGO

Celebes Sea

Philippines

Feet	Meters	
9843	3000	Mountains
6582	2000	Uplands
3281	1000	
1640	500	Lowlands

Elevation

N

▲ Mountain peak

—— International border

0   150 Miles

0   150 KM

CHINA

VIETNAM

Taiwan

PACIFIC OCEAN

PHILIPPINES

INDONESIA

INDIAN OCEAN

AUSTRALIA

1000 Miles

1000 KM

The 1991 eruption of Mount Pinatubo was the second-largest volcanic blast of the twentieth century. The eruption sent more than 20 billion tons (18 billion metric tons) of ash into the air. The ash, which spread around the planet, blocked out so much sunlight that it lowered the average global temperature and affected weather systems around the world.

Mount Mayon, another active volcano, reaches a height of 8,284 feet (2,525 m) in southeastern Luzon. This volcano's large cone is often hidden in water vapor that rises from the crater. A major earthquake in 1990 awoke Mount Pinatubo in central Luzon, which had been dormant for six hundred years. The volcano erupted in 1991, burying 200,000 acres (81,000 hectares) of land in thick ash.

MINDANAO The second-largest island of the Philippines, Mindanao is shaped like an irregular triangle. Its coastline has many bays and inlets. Just off the eastern coast of this island is the Philippine Trench—a huge depression in the Philippine Sea. At its deepest point, the trench descends 34,578 feet (10,539 m) below the water's surface.

On the eastern coast of Mindanao, the Diuata Mountains rise to more than 6,000 feet (1,830 m). The Agusan River valley extends for about 50 miles (80 km) west of these mountains. In central Mindanao, the Katanglad Mountains reach almost 9,000 feet (2,700 m) above sea level. Located near the city of Davao, Mount Apo—an active volcano that rises to 9,692 feet (2,954 m)—is the highest mountain in the Philippines. The Cotabato Valley reaches westward from the center of the island, and the Zamboanga Mountains stand on a peninsula that juts into the Sulu Sea.

THE VISAYAN ISLANDS Composed of more than six thousand islands, the Visayan Islands have seven principal landmasses. The easternmost of the seven is Samar, which has low, rugged mountains covered with dense rain forests. Samar receives heavy rainfall from annual typhoons (hurricane-like storms that form in the western Pacific). Leyte, lying southwest of Samar, has mountains that run through the center of the island and rise to more than 4,000 feet (1,220 m). With coastal areas wider than those of Samar, Leyte supports fields of coconuts, corn, rice, and abaca (a plant from which rope is made).

Centrally located in the Visayas, Cebu Island is one of the most populous of the Philippine Islands. A long, narrow landmass with central mountains extending its entire length, Cebu reaches its highest point at 3,324 feet (1,013 m) above sea level. Cebu has very limited

level land, which restricts agricultural activities on the island. South of Cebu, the round island of Bohol has a large lowland area and mountains that reach an elevation of 2,600 feet (800 m). Bohol's smooth coastline offers few good places for ships to anchor.

Lying west of Cebu is Negros Island, with a largely mountainous topography except for coastal plains to the north. The island's highest peak is Mount Canlaon, an active volcano that rises 8,070 feet (2,460 m) above sea level. Volcanic lava, which has spread over the island during centuries of frequent eruptions, contains nutrients that have enriched the soil of Negros.

Panay lies northwest of Negros and is the westernmost of the Visayan Islands. Panay's mountains run parallel to the western coast, and Mount Nangtud (6,724 ft. or 2,049 m) is the tallest. A feature of central Panay is a large lowland area, which is matched in the southeast by the Iloilo Plain. Masbate is the northernmost major island of the Visayas. Low mountains cover Masbate, which is the Philippines' main gold-producing region.

THE CHOCOLATE HILLS

The island of Bohol features the Chocolate Hills (above). All 1,268 of these hills are the same rounded shape and stand between 100 and 160 feet (30 and 50 m) tall. The grass covering the hills is green for much of the year, but it turns the color of chocolate at the end of the dry season. Geologists do not know how the Chocolate Hills formed. Local legend says that long ago a young giant named Arogo fell in love with a human girl named Aloya. When she died, the broken-hearted giant cried. His huge tears fell to the ground and hardened into the Chocolate Hills.

◉ Rivers and Lakes

The Philippine Islands have many rivers, most of which are short and swift. The heavy rainfall that accompanies the region's monsoons (seasonal winds) often floods the rivers. Luzon and Mindanao contain the longest and most important rivers.

Much of the Cagayan River in northern Luzon is navigable by boat. As it flows northward along its 220-mile (354 km) course, this river irrigates the 50-mile-wide (80 km wide) valley between the Sierra Madre and the Cordillera Central. After passing the coastal city of Aparri, the Cagayan empties into the Babuyan Channel. The Pampanga River, another major waterway on Luzon, begins in the Caraballo Mountains and flows south for 120 miles (190 km) into Manila Bay. The central plain, which receives the Pampanga's waters, is one of the most fertile areas in the Philippines. Beginning in the Cordillera Central, the Agno River turns west and irrigates another wide plain before emptying into Lingayen Gulf.

One of the world's longest navigable underground rivers flows for more than 5 miles (8 km) beneath the mountainous island of Palawan. The river winds through a limestone cave that features huge chambers and tall cliffs, as well as stalactites, stalagmites, and other rock formations. Visitors can explore the waterway by tour boat.

In eastern Mindanao, the Agusan River extends 240 miles (390 km) as it travels north to Butuan Bay. The fertile valley that the Agusan creates is 50 miles (80 km) wide and supports large rice and corn crops. The Mindanao River begins in the central part of the island and flows north and west for more than 100 (160 km) miles before reaching Illana Bay. Small boats navigate much of the Mindanao River, and the waterway's tributaries make the surrounding territory a highly productive agricultural area.

Although it has many small lakes, the Philippines contains only three lakes of considerable size. Laguna de Bay lies in central Luzon near Manila. The largest lake in the Philippines, it covers 344 square miles (891 sq. km). The 14-mile-long (23 km long) Pasig River carries overflow from the lake through the capital city into Manila Bay. About 40 miles (64 km) south of Manila is the 94-square-mile (243 sq. km) Lake Taal, which is situated within the collapsed cone of a dead volcano. The active volcano Mount Taal forms an island in the center of the lake. Mindanao's Lake Lanao sits on a plateau north of the Katanglad Mountains and occupies an

Mount Taal, one of the smallest and most active volcanoes in the world, rises in the center of **Lake Taal.**

area of 131 square miles (339 sq. km). The Agus River provides Lake Lanao's outlet to the sea.

Climate

The Philippines has a rainy season and a dry season. The weather on the islands changes depending on the direction of the monsoons. When the southwest monsoon blows from May to November, the Philippine Islands receive plenty of rain from the moisture-laden winds. In lowland areas, the average rainfall is more than 80 inches (200 centimeter) during this season, while in the mountains, up to 150 inches (380 cm) are common. Although many fields often flood, farmers who grow rice use the floodwater to irrigate their crops. Temperatures hover around 80°F (27°C) during the rainy season.

In December the direction of the wind changes, and the northeast monsoon starts to blow. Lasting until April, the northeast monsoon causes several months of cooler weather for much of the nation. Manila averages 75°F (24°C) in January, and in some areas, the temperature occasionally falls below 70°F (21°C). By April, however, Manila's temperatures are back in the low 80s°F (less than 30°C), and highs of more than 100°F (38°C) are often recorded in other areas of the country.

From June until October, the Philippines also experiences a typhoon season. Typhoons are large, slow-moving storms that bring heavy rains. Winds that reach speeds of 150 miles per hour (240 km/h) accompany the storms. A dozen or more typhoons sweep the Philippines each year. Five or six of them hit the islands with destructive force, ruining homes and sometimes killing people and livestock. Typhoons most often affect northern Luzon and the eastern Visayas.

Natural Resources and Environmental Challenges

The Philippines is rich in mineral resources, with large deposits of copper, chromite, and gold. Other minerals include coal, cobalt, gypsum, iron, salt, nickel, silver, and sulfur. Workers also mine valuable building stone, such as limestone and marble. Deposits of petroleum and natural gas lie offshore, providing significant potential for energy production.

The underground fault lines that cause earthquakes and volcanic eruptions in the Philippines also produce heat. This heat creates hot water and steam that is tapped to make geothermal energy. The Philippines is one of the largest producers of geothermal energy in the world. The nation's rivers provide hydropower energy.

Fish are one of the Philippines largest natural resources, but their numbers in the country's coastal waters have steadily dropped due to overfishing. The government has worked to regulate the number of boats working in overfished areas because further depletion of the fish stock could greatly reduce catches in the future. But a lack of funds has limited the government's efforts. In recent years, the government encouraged Filipinos to develop deep-water fishing instead of relying on the nation's traditional coastal fishing grounds. Still, the outlook for the nation's fishing industry is bleak, and some fishers have turned to more extreme methods, such as blast fishing. Using underwater explosives, fishers stun or kill fish to make them float to the surface. These blasts are causing great harm to the delicate coral reefs that lie in the coastal waters.

Land in the Philippines is also suffering. Thick forests that once dominated the Philippine landscape cover about one-fourth of the country these days. Uncontrolled logging has destroyed large areas of the country's rain forests. Without trees to anchor the soil, erosion occurs and is especially serious during the height of the monsoon rains. Farmers who cut and burn vegetation to clear new fields for cultivation have also damaged the nation's timber resources. Conservation and reforestation efforts sponsored by the government began in the 1970s but have proceeded slowly.

Flora and Fauna

Tropical rain forests cover the slopes of many Philippine mountains and some lowland areas. Sunlight, warmth, rain, and fertile soil cause some trees in these forests to grow 150 feet (45 m) tall, creating a leafy canopy. Beneath the shade of the treetops, vines, epiphytes (air plants), and climbing palms thrive. Pine forests are common at higher elevations. Stands of Philippine mahogany, banyan (part of the mulberry family), and molave (a tree with hard, yellow wood) also grow on the archipelago.

Cogon—a type of thick grass—grows on many of the plateaus throughout the islands. The grass forms a dense turf and has roots that are highly resistant to fire. Bamboo plants sprout along many of the islands' coasts and rivers. The Philippines' national flower is the sampaguita orchid, one of more than nine thousand flowering plants in the country.

The islands host a variety of animals. Small, wild buffalo known as tamarau roam the mountains of Mindoro. Tarsiers—mammals that live mostly in trees and have owl-like eyes—probably came to the islands centuries ago from India. Mouse deer—a species of small, red deer—live on Palawan Island. Water buffalo, called carabao, are the main domestic animals in the Philippines. The forests of the country contain many varieties of monkeys.

Once found throughout the region, crocodiles now inhabit only remote regions of Palawan and Mindanao. Pythons, water snakes, and other varieties of snakes are common throughout the islands. Lizards also live in the Philippines. Geckos eat insects. Young Filipinos sometimes keep these small lizards as pets. Monitor lizards find suitable

The **sampaguita orchid** is the national flower of the Philippines. The **tarsier** is the world's oldest surviving primate. Each of a tarsier's eyes is bigger than its brain and cannot move in the eye socket. To compensate, a tarsier can swivel its head nearly 180 degrees in each direction, like an owl.

SWIMMING WITH WHALE SHARKS

Large numbers of migrating whale sharks feed on plankton in the waters off Donsol, a village on southern Luzon. Known by the villagers as *butanding*, the whale shark is the largest fish in the world, measuring up to 45 feet (14 m) long and weighing about 125 tons (113 metric tons). After a newspaper carried a story about Donsol's whale sharks in 1998, poachers soon arrived to hunt the silver-spotted animals. The local government quickly passed an ordinance that outlawed catching whale sharks. Since then travelers from around the world have come to Donsol to see the famous creatures. Gentle and friendly, whale sharks do not seem to mind if people swim alongside them. Snorkelers regularly take to the water to see these amazing fish up close.

habitats throughout the countryside. The Philippine eagle—the world's largest eagle species—preys upon geckos and monitor lizards. Parrots, found predominantly on Palawan, have brightly colored feathers and are often exported to other countries as pets.

◉ Cities

METRO MANILA The cities of the Philippines contain approximately 48 percent of the nation's population. Manila is the capital of the Philippines. It is also the commercial hub, principal port city, and financial center of the country. Located in central Luzon, Manila grew from more than a dozen small cities and towns that were clustered along Manila Bay. The city itself has a population of nearly 1.6 million people, while more than 10 million people live in the wider metropolitan area, called Metro Manila.

The Pasig River divides Manila in half. South of the river lies Intramuros, an old walled city that was built by the Spanish. Farther south is Rizal Park (also known as Luneta)—a large, open space that serves as a central meeting place for the city's inhabitants. Among the neighborhoods north of the river is Tondo, a poor community with overcrowded, makeshift housing. Manila also is the site of Malacañang Palace, the president's official residence.

Bordering Manila on the northeast is Quezon City, part of Metro Manila. With a population of more than 2 million, Quezon City is the most populous city in the Philippines. Quezon City served as the nation's capital from 1948 until 1976. Although Manila is the capital, many government offices continue to operate from Quezon City. The central campus of the University of the Philippines is also located in Quezon City.

Cebu City is one of the oldest cities in the Philippines.

OTHER CITIES Davao, the largest Philippine city in area, lies on the southeastern coast of Mindanao Island and is one of the fastest-growing cities in the nation. With more than 1 million people, Davao draws many immigrants from other Philippine islands. These Filipinos seek jobs as farmworkers in the surrounding region. Coconuts move through Davao's port to be exported worldwide.

Cebu City, on the eastern coast of the island of Cebu, has a thriving harbor. Most of the imports and exports of the Visayan Islands arrive and depart through this port. With a population of more than 700,000 people, Cebu is one of the Philippines' largest cities. Among the first Spanish settlements in the archipelago, Cebu City contains sixteenth-century Fort San Pedro, as well as many Spanish-style churches. Several universities are located within the city, including Southwestern University, which was founded in 1950.

Another major port city is Iloilo on southeastern Panay Island. Because pirates often raided the settlement during the 1700s and 1800s, residents built many stone watchtowers and defensive forts. Iloilo is a major agricultural trading center with more than 400,000 inhabitants. The city is also a commercial center for the textile industry.

For more information about the Philippines' cities, including what there is to see and do in each city, what the weather is like there, and more, visit www.vgsbooks.com for links.

HISTORY AND GOVERNMENT

In Luzon's Cagayan Valley, archaeologists have discovered stone tools and remains of campsites that belonged to the ancient inhabitants of the Philippine Islands. These materials date from 250,000 years ago, when the region was still connected to Asia by land.

Waves of ethnic groups from different parts of Asia came to the Philippines by an overland route. About twenty-five thousand years ago, the Aeta people—hunters who used bows and arrows—arrived in the territory.

Other people migrated from the neighboring island of Borneo about twelve thousand years later. These newcomers planted and harvested crops in addition to hunting for their food. Roughly twelve thousand years ago, sheets of ice (glaciers), covering large areas of the earth's surface, melted. The water submerged the land routes that connected the Philippines to other parts of Asia. From this time on, the Philippines were islands.

Between 1500 and 500 B.C., Malays and people from present-day China and Vietnam came to the region in oceangoing canoes. As these

newcomers settled along the coasts, the inhabitants who already lived in the archipelago moved to the interior of the islands. The new arrivals used tools and weapons of polished stone and grouped their dwellings in villages. The newer Malay immigrants introduced carabao as work animals. These Malays and their descendants also cultivated rice on terraces cut into the mountainsides of northern Luzon. Malay people continued to come to the islands in large numbers for many centuries.

○ Contact with Ancient Kingdoms

The location of the Philippines between the Indian and the Pacific oceans made it a convenient stopping place for sea traders. Many merchants came from the kingdom of Sri Vijaya, which was situated southwest of the Philippines on the island of Sumatra. By the A.D. 600s, Sri Vijaya was a major Pacific trading power.

Sri Vijaya controlled many of the sea routes throughout Southeast Asian waters, including those through the Philippines. Sri Vijayan

About five thousand years ago, inhabitants of present-day Luzon created rock engravings of human and animal figures. Known as the Angono Petroglyphs, these drawings on the back wall of a rock shelter make up the oldest known rock art in the Philippines. At one time, 127 engravings existed. But due to weather elements and vandalism, many of the drawings have disappeared.

control of trade in the Philippines and in the rest of Southeast Asia lasted for about five hundred years. Besides naming the Visayan Islands after themselves, the Sri Vijayans also influenced the religion of the archipelago. They introduced Filipinos to Buddhism—a faith inspired by Gautama Buddha in India during the sixth century B.C.

The Majapahit kingdom, which followed the Hindu religion, arose on the island of Java in the late 1200s. Soon Majapahit princes replaced the Sri Vijayans as controllers of the sea-lanes in the Philippines. Although the Majapahit leaders did not deliberately try to introduce Hinduism into the regions they controlled, many elements of their Hindu culture came to the islands. For example, the Filipino *barong*—a distinctive shirt—is an adaptation of a garment worn by Hindus from southern India. Filipinos also adopted many words from Sanskrit, the language of Hinduism.

ARAB AND CHINESE TRADERS During the eras of Sri Vijayan and Majapahit influence in the Philippines, Arab and Chinese traders also came to the islands. By the fourteenth century, Arabs had arrived in the southern part of the archipelago. They had success in spreading Islam—a religion founded in the seventh century A.D. in Arabia. By the middle of the fifteenth century, many people on the southern islands, especially Mindanao, had become Muslims (followers of Islam). Muslim traders from India, Malacca, and Borneo also came to the Philippines and helped to spread Islam.

Meanwhile, Chinese merchants approached the Philippines from the north. Landing most often on Luzon, these traders exchanged silk and porcelain for Philippine timber and gold. During the Chinese Ming era (1368–1644), the merchants established settlements on Luzon. The port of Lingayen, for example, took its name from a powerful Chinese trader called Lin Gaiyen.

At the beginning of the fifteenth century, Chinese influence was so strong that Chinese leaders governed several of the northern islands. The Chinese clashed with Muslims from the south, however, and eventually lost many of their settlements on the islands. By the start of the 1500s, Muslims had extended their influence throughout much of Luzon.

Spanish Explorers

Beginning in the 1500s, European explorers searched for a short route to Asia's rich spice markets. Ferdinand Magellan, a Portuguese-born navigator who sailed under the flag of Spain, traveled through Southeast Asian waters. His voyage took him to present-day Malaysia and Indonesia and on to Homonhon, a small island south of Leyte, in 1521. Traveling on to nearby Limasawa and Cebu, Magellan met friendly residents of these islands. The local people welcomed the Europeans and, at first, agreed to adopt the Christian religion.

Not everyone Magellan met, however, was friendly. Lapu-Lapu, ruler of the island of Mactan, refused to accept European ways or to be ruled by the advancing explorers. Magellan set out to conquer Lapu-Lapu and his followers, but Lapu-Lapu's warriors easily defeated the Europeans. Magellan was killed in the fighting on April 27, 1521. Survivors of the battle left the islands and continued their westward voyage around the world.

Magellan lands in the Philippines in 1521. Magellan's crew formed close relationships with some of the islanders and took great pride in converting many to their Christian religion.

NATIONAL HERO

Filipinos consider the Mactan chieftain Lapu-Lapu a brave warrior and their first national hero for fighting off Spanish attempts to conquer his people. In his honor, the Cebuano people of Mactan Island erected a statue *(above)* and a church. They also named one of their cities Lapu-Lapu City. The chieftain's image also appears on the one-centavo coin used throughout the Philippines.

Despite this early defeat, the Spanish continued to explore the Pacific. Ruy Lopez de Villalobos landed on Mindanao in February 1545. Villalobos wanted to strengthen the Spanish claim to the islands by establishing permanent settlements in the archipelago. He named the islands las Islas Filipinas (Philippine Islands), after the Spanish king, Phillip II. Lack of provisions and hostility from the local inhabitants hindered his plans. Nevertheless, the Spanish established their first colony at San Miguel, later known as Cebu City, on Cebu Island. Developed in 1565 by Miguel Lopez de Legazpi, the Spanish settlement housed four hundred soldiers and several missionaries.

EARLY SPANISH RULE Although the inhabitants strongly resented losing their independence, Legazpi and his troops slowly brought the islanders under Spanish power. Occasionally more soldiers and missionaries arrived from Spain to reinforce Legazpi's efforts.

Many of the inhabitants of the archipelago became Christians at the urging of the missionaries. The Muslims (whom the Spanish called Moros) were the most difficult group for the soldiers to overcome and for the missionaries to convert. Large numbers of Moros in Mindanao successfully resisted the Spaniards.

In 1571 Legazpi and his forces occupied Manila. The small population of Moros on Luzon fought the Spanish troops but eventually lost. Igorots—members of ethnic groups from the hills and mountains on Luzon—also resisted Spanish expansion and were difficult for the Europeans to conquer.

After defeating most of the resistant islanders, the colonizers made the region useful to their expanding empire. They established Manila as the central port for ships that carried silver from South America across the Pacific. Traders from China exchanged porcelain, silk, and textiles for Spanish gold at Manila's port. These early colonizers did little to develop the Philippine economy beyond introducing maize (corn) and improving the irrigation system in the region's rice fields.

Spanish Occupation

The Spanish ruled the Philippines by expanding the system of organization that the people of the islands already used. The basic unit of government was the village, or *barangay*. Each village had a *datu* (ruler) who was chosen by informal agreement among the local residents. Roman Catholic priests lived in the barangays as missionaries and as representatives of the colonial administration. In these roles, they were able to strongly influence the selection of the datu.

THE PARIAN

In the late 1500s, the Spanish governor became alarmed at the growth of the Chinese community in Intramuros, the former Spanish capital that lies within the modern-day city of Manila. To better collect taxes and keep a closer eye on the Chinese, Spanish leaders segregated them from the rest of the population into the Parian, or marketplace. At dawn the gates of the Parian opened and the residents of Intramuros shopped for goods such as silk and porcelain from traders known as the Sangley. In 1683 the Parian was transferred to the district of Binondo, which is still known as Chinatown.

The indirect rule of the Philippines by the Spanish missionaries was not successful in every region of the country. Diego Silang, a Filipino leader from northern Luzon, rebelled against the Spanish in 1762 and set up his own government in the city of Vigan. The Moros on the southern islands raided Spanish military outposts and achieved independence in their own territories.

In the late eighteenth century, the Spanish used force to regain control over many of the rebellious groups in the country. The Europeans also introduced agricultural reforms. Administrators encouraged Filipino farmers to grow export crops such as abaca (a plant whose fibers are used to make Manila hemp), tea, and tobacco. The colonial government established complete control over the sale of tobacco. This monopoly brought great wealth to Spanish officials.

In the early 1800s, the Spanish opened the Philippines to trade with merchants from Great Britain, the United States, France, and other nations. Sugarcane, abaca, and tobacco became major exports and helped to develop the Philippine economy.

Early Revolts

Although the colony's economy grew, most Filipinos did not benefit from increased trade. Missionaries, Spanish officials, and a few wealthy Filipinos owned most of the land and controlled commerce. The majority of Filipinos worked as tenant farmers and paid high rents to local landowners for the use of the land.

The dissatisfaction of the Philippine population deepened, and several communities rebelled. The Ilocanos, an ethnic group from Luzon, revolted in 1807 when government officials took control of the region's wine-making industry. In 1841 many Filipinos joined their fellow islander Apolonario de la Cruz in an armed revolt on Luzon against Spanish oppression. Throughout the nineteenth century, many groups of Filipinos pressured Spanish leaders for economic reform and more political freedom. Lacking education or an official voice in colonial affairs, these Filipinos made little progress in improving conditions.

Among the small number of Filipinos who had studied at universities either in Manila or in Europe was José Rizal. By the end of the 1800s, he had become the most famous supporter of Philippine independence. A doctor and writer, Rizal established the Filipino League in 1891. His organization was dedicated to ending abuses of Spanish power, such as forcing laborers to work on plantations. The league's goal was to establish a self-governing Philippine nation.

Spanish officials exiled Rizal to northwestern Mindanao soon after he started the organization. When Rizal became a popular symbol of Filipino resistance, the Spanish executed him. Without Rizal's leadership, the Filipino League dissolved.

The name *Katipunan* is actually a shorter version of the secret society's official name. In the Tagalog language (the language Filipino is based on), the name is *Kataastaasang, Kagalanggalangang Katipunan ng mga Anak ng Bayan*, which is roughly translated in English as "the Highest and Most Respected Society of the Sons and Daughters of the Land."

Revolution and War

In 1892 Andres Bonifacio founded the Katipunan. This secret organization dedicated itself to overthrowing the Spanish colonizers through armed force. In 1896 thirty thousand members of the Katipunan launched attacks against the Spanish.

Only one rebel leader, Emilio Aguinaldo, successfully led his troops against the Spanish. He replaced Bonifacio as the Katipunan leader in 1897. Although the

While rebel **Emilio Aguinaldo** was in exile in Hong Kong, he designed the current national flag of the Philippines.

Spanish recaptured most of their territory, they failed to overcome Aguinaldo's forces. The Spanish moved to negotiate peace with the Katipunan. Aguinaldo signed the Pact of Biac-na-Bato with the colonizers. In the treaty, the Spanish promised self-rule for the Filipinos within three years if Aguinaldo would go into exile. In December 1897, the rebel leader sailed for Hong Kong.

Meanwhile, other parts of Spain's empire were rebelling. When the Caribbean island of Cuba declared independence from Spain, the United States and Spain confronted each other in the Spanish-American War in early 1898.

Among the colonial prizes at stake in the war was the Philippines. Commodore George Dewey brought the U.S. Navy from Hong Kong into Manila Bay in April 1898, and by May 1, he had defeated the Spanish naval force. Aguinaldo returned from Hong Kong and led his Katipunan soldiers in the fight against the Spanish. In return for Katipunan assistance, the U.S. government promised independence for the Philippines.

Combined U.S. and Katipunan forces defeated the Spanish in August 1898. Later that year, the Treaty of Paris officially concluded the war between the United States and Spain. Under the treaty, the United States gained control of the Philippines, Guam, and Puerto Rico and in return gave Spain $20 million.

To many islanders, U.S. occupation was not an improvement over Spanish rule. Aguinaldo and many of the Filipino people resisted the U.S. presence. Rejecting any form of colonial control, Aguinaldo

The May 1, 1898, **battle in Manila Bay** destroyed the entire Spanish fleet without the loss of American life or serious damage to any U.S. ships. To learn more about the battle and the Spanish-American War, visit www.vgsbooks.com for links.

proclaimed national independence in 1898. Until his capture in 1901, he led armed resistance against U.S. forces. Remnants of his army continued to fight for another year without their leader.

U.S. Rule

In the early twentieth century, U.S. president William McKinley said that the United States did not intend to possess the Philippine Islands permanently. The United States accepted the idea of eventual independence for the Filipino people after a period of preparation for self-rule. As a result, education became a major focus for the U.S. administration of the islands. More than six hundred teachers from the United States came to the Philippines to help establish schools. Hundreds of U.S. citizens financially supported the University of the Philippines when it opened in Manila in 1908.

From the beginning of the period of U.S. control, Filipinos participated in governing the territory, although not fully enough for those who eagerly awaited national independence. Manuel Luis Quezon y Molina, Sergio Osmeña, and Manuel Roxas y Acuña were Filipino leaders who pushed U.S. officials for more self-rule in the Philippines.

As a result of Philippine concerns, the U.S. Congress passed the Tydings-McDuffie

"Our noble aspirations for nationhood, long cherished and arduously contended for by our people, will be realized."

—Manuel Roxas y Acuña

Act in 1934. The act provided for a Philippine constitution and for the election of a legislature and a president by the Philippine people. The Philippines would govern itself internally, but the United States would retain control of foreign affairs and defense for a period of ten years. The Philippine people ratified the constitution in May 1935, and in November Quezon was elected president.

WORLD WAR II On December 10, 1941, three days after World War II (1939–1945) began in the Pacific, Japanese troops invaded the Philippines. Philippine and U.S. forces fought against the Japanese for several months, but the invaders pushed them into the Bataan Peninsula and onto Corregidor Island. On May 6, 1942, the commonwealth of the Philippines surrendered, and the Japanese occupied the country. Quezon and other government leaders fled to Washington, D.C., to establish a government-in-exile.

The Japanese took most of the nation's rice to feed their soldiers throughout the Pacific, and many people in the Philippines starved. Most Filipinos refused to cooperate with harsh Japanese rule, and many actively resisted the enemy through guerrilla warfare (attacks by small combat groups).

THE BATAAN DEATH MARCH

During World War II, Japanese forces captured seventy thousand U.S. and Filipino soldiers. Lacking the trucks to transport them, the Japanese forced their prisoners of war to march to a prison camp. On April 9, 1942, starting from the southern end of the Bataan Peninsula on Luzon, the soldiers marched 55 miles (88 km) to San Fernando. Trains took the prisoners to Capas. From there, the soldiers walked the last 8 miles (13 km) to a concentration camp. During this forced march, the Japanese captors starved U.S. and Filipino soldiers and often kicked or beat them. Japanese soldiers killed many who fell. Only fifty-four thousand of the prisoners reached the camp. Between seven thousand and ten thousand soldiers died, while the rest were able to escape into the jungle. Every year on April 9, Filipinos remember the captured soldiers on Bataan Day, a national holiday in the Philippines.

Philippine Independence

Quezon died while leading the Philippine government-in-exile in the United States. Sergio Osmeña, his vice president, succeeded him and brought the government back to Manila in 1945. That year Japan surrendered, officially ending World War II. Manuel Roxas y Acuña won the presidential election held in April 1946. As chief executive, he began to rebuild the nation after the destruction of the war.

Filipinos in Manila celebrate the anniversary of their **independence** from the United States.

A DAY OF INDEPENDENCE

When the Philippines gained its independence on July 4, 1946, Katipunan leader Emilio Aguinaldo saw his lifelong goal achieved. But he believed the true date of independence was June 12, 1898, the day he had raised the Philippine flag and declared the country free of foreign rule. Many years later, to promote nationalism, President Diosdado Macapagal changed Independence Day from July 4 to June 12. Aguinaldo considered this action a great victory for Katipunan revolutionaries and left his sickbed to celebrate his country's independence sixty-two years after he had first declared it.

In accordance with the Tydings-McDuffie Act, the United States withdrew its authority over the Philippines. On July 4, 1946, the Republic of the Philippines achieved full independence. The U.S. government supported the new nation with economic assistance. In return, the Philippine government allowed the United States to keep military bases on the islands.

Along with the difficulties of rebuilding the nation after the war, the Filipino government also faced a challenge from Communist rebels. Called the People's Liberation Army (or Huks, a Tagalog abbreviation), the revolutionaries operated in central Luzon. The Huks wanted farmers' and workers' groups to have authority over land and industry. They believed that the Communist principles of shared landownership and equal distribution of income should guide these organizations.

In the late 1940s and early 1950s, Huk guerrillas attacked government forces. The rebels gained support from many local people who were suffering from difficult postwar economic conditions. Ramón

Magsaysay, the secretary of defense, led the Philippine army against the Huks. After his election as president in 1953, he effectively halted the Huk rebellion.

Besides overcoming the Huks, President Magsaysay was able to gather enough support from the Philippine legislature to pass land reform laws. These measures broke up some of the large tracts of land that wealthy Filipinos owned. The government redistributed much of this land to the tenant farm families who had worked the fields for decades.

Under Magsaysay's administration, foreign investment grew and the economy improved. Magsaysay, known for his fairness and effectiveness, died in a plane crash in 1957. The administrations that followed attempted to break up even more of the huge tracts held by wealthy landowners. But landowners were politically powerful, and they blocked the reforms that these governments introduced.

Diosdado Macapagal, who became president in 1961, started another land reform program but met with limited success. Dissatisfaction with Macapagal's leadership grew. In the 1965 election, Ferdinand Marcos—a member of the Philippine legislature—won the presidency.

The Marcos Era

During his first term as president, Marcos advocated two programs that won him loyalty from many Filipinos. One was an agricultural program focused on developing a new strain of rice. The rice would yield larger crops and provide more food for the country. The other was a public works program that oversaw the completion of many projects.

The new rice crop that **Ferdinand Marcos** introduced to the country was known as miracle rice because it was disease resistant. This and other measures made Marcos a popular president and the first to win two terms in office.

Marcos won a second term in 1969, and his administration faced new difficulties. Economic progress slowed, and the standard of living for the average Filipino fell. Muslim groups on Mindanao grew increasingly resentful of the growing Christian population on the island. Extremists organized the Moro National Liberation Front (MNLF). These radical Muslims armed themselves and sought self-rule in the southern islands.

Another problem for Marcos and his government was a reborn Communist presence, called the New People's Army (NPA). Members of this group wanted more land reform and a political revolution. These rebels had especially strong support on the main island of Luzon.

During these years, Marcos supported the U.S. role in the Vietnam War (1957–1975), in which U.S. forces joined with South Vietnam to fight against North Vietnam. The U.S. military bases at Subic Bay and Clark Air Base on Luzon were important to the U.S. effort in Vietnam. Many Filipinos recognized the U.S. military presence as a continuation of the colonial bond between the two countries. Filipino nationalists regarded the United States with hostility.

Filipino students demonstrated in 1971 against the presence of the U.S. bases in the Philippines. Rally leaders also spoke against Marcos's failure to achieve economic reforms. As they tried to break up a demonstration in May 1972, national police killed dozens and

The military commanders of the **Moro National Liberation Front** meet to plan revolutionary activities in the late 1960s.

wounded hundreds of protesters. In September 1972, a group of assassins unsuccessfully tried to kill the secretary of national defense, Juan Ponce Enrile. These violent events contributed to an atmosphere of unrest within the country.

MARTIAL LAW In response to increasing difficulties, Marcos declared martial law (rule by the military) in 1972. Marcos took away the right of Filipinos to meet for political purposes, dissolved the constitution and the Congress, and controlled the news media. He also limited the civil rights of Filipino citizens and arrested many of his opponents. Marcos exercised absolute power and only rarely sought public support through referendums (nationwide votes) on specific programs.

In 1973 a new constitution gave Marcos free rein to rule the country and an unlimited term of office. Marcos shared his power with a small group of supporters—including his wife, Imelda. During the 1970s, many Filipinos began to recognize that the Marcos administration was unable to solve the economic and political problems of the country. Others suspected Marcos of taking huge amounts of money from the foreign loans made to the nation. (In 1988 the United States charged Marcos with stealing millions of dollars that it had loaned to the Philippines for economic development.)

Under increasing pressure from the Filipino Roman Catholic Church to reestablish democratic elections and to observe human rights, Marcos ended martial law in 1981. Marcos won the presidency again that year in an election that observers said was dishonest. Many Filipinos began calling for a change of national leadership.

BENIGNO AND CORAZON AQUINO One of Marcos's opponents who had been arrested under martial law was Benigno Aquino. In 1977 a court established by Marcos had falsely convicted Aquino of murder and possession of firearms and had sentenced him to death. Filipinos believed that the conviction was politically motivated, and public pressure forced Marcos to lift the execution order. In 1980 the government released Aquino, giving him permission to travel to the United States for medical treatment. The opposition leader remained in exile for three years.

"I have carefully weighed the virtues and the faults of the Filipino, and I have come to the conclusion that he is worth dying for."

— Benigno Aquino

In 1983 Aquino was determined to return to the Philippines to lead a movement for democratic reform. Although his closest advisers—including his wife, Corazon—discouraged his return to the Philippines, Aquino left the United States in August 1983. Soon after exiting the airplane at Manila Airport, he was assassinated.

Many people believed Marcos was behind Aquino's assassination. Marcos felt pressure to restore confidence in his administration and to reopen the democratic channels of government. In November 1985, Marcos called for a presidential election to be held in February 1986. Although she had little political experience, Corazon Aquino became the main candidate opposing Marcos.

A national commission with strong ties to Marcos counted the votes in the 1986 election, but several international observers also kept track of the tally. When the government commission proclaimed Marcos the winner, these observers accused him and the commission of falsifying the election results. Without popular or international support, Marcos resigned, ending his twenty-one-year rule of the Philippines. Corazon Aquino took office on February 25, 1986. Marcos and his family fled to Hawaii a few weeks later.

◎ Restoring Democracy

After becoming president of the Philippines, Corazon Aquino quickly restored freedom of the press and the full rights of citizens. In February 1987, 76 percent of eligible voters approved a new constitution. Aquino focused on ridding the government of corruption. She also

Filipinos rally in support of **constitutional ratification.**

worked to heal the fractious country, but she was unsuccessful in making peace with the NPA and the MNLF rebel groups. Although economic reform was one of Aquino's priorities, attempts by military officers to overthrow her administration hampered progress.

In 1991 Aquino faced negotiations with the United States over extending a treaty to keep U.S. air bases in the Philippines. Although the bases contributed greatly to the Philippine economy, many Filipinos considered the bases an unwelcome reminder of U.S. rule. Then disaster struck the country when Mount Pinatubo erupted on Luzon, killing more than one thousand people and displacing thousands more. The blast also buried Clark Air Base in ash, making it inoperable. When the air base treaty failed to pass in the Philippine Senate, the United States pulled out of the Subic Bay base as well.

In 1992 Filipinos elected defense minister Fidel Ramos president. To many, the peaceful transfer of power from Aquino to Ramos affirmed democracy in the Philippines. Under Ramos the government legalized the Communist Party, which reduced support for the NPA. The government also signed a peace agreement with the MNLF, which designated a region of self-rule for Muslims in the southern Philippines. This region is known as the Autonomous Region of Muslim Mindanao (ARMM). Two other Muslim rebel groups—the Moro Islamic Liberation Front (MILF) and Abu Sayyaf—continued to

Ash and smoke billow out of **Mount Pinatubo** as it erupts in June 1991. The column of ash rose 25 miles (40 km) into the air. The eruption had as much force as a nuclear detonation, causing earthquakes, thunder, and lightning, and lowering the height of the mountain by 984 feet (300 m).

fight the government. Ramos also made significant economic progress for the Philippines through banking, tax, and trade reforms.

Recent Events

Vice President Joseph Estrada won the 1998 presidential election with overwhelming support. During his campaign, he promised to reduce poverty and crack down on crime. In 2000, however, Estrada was accused of corruption, including taking millions of dollars in bribes. In January 2001, after widespread public demonstrations calling for his resignation, Estrada stepped aside. Vice President Gloria Macapagal-Arroyo, the daughter of former president Diosdado Macapagal, rose to the presidency. She pledged to unify the country and establish economic reforms to fight growing poverty.

Under Arroyo, the Philippine government continued to deal with threats from separatists as well as growing concerns of terrorism. In 2001 the MILF signed a cease-fire agreement and began talks with the government. Although sporadic fighting broke out, the peace process proceeded. In June 2003, the MILF formally renounced terrorism. The Philippine government refused to negotiate with the smaller and more extreme Abu Sayyaf, however, because its tactics included kidnapping foreigners for ransom. The Philippine government, along with the U.S. government, also accused Abu Sayyaf of ties to the Islamic terrorist organization al-Qaeda and its leader, Osama bin Laden.

In 2004 Arroyo won the 2004 presidential election, defeating popular movie actor Fernando Poe Jr. She vowed to wipe out Abu Sayyaf, which had recently stepped up its terrorist tactics. In February 2004, the group set off a bomb aboard a Philippine passenger ferry, killing more than one hundred people. Fourteen people were killed and

Gloria Macapagal-Arroyo was a senator and the vice president before she became president of the Philippines in 2001. In 1995, her second term as a senator, she received 16 million votes, the highest number in any election in Philippine history. And when she became vice president in 1998, her 13 million votes were the highest in any presidential or vice-presidential election.

more than fifty injured that December when a bomb ripped through a marketplace in the city of General Santos on Mindanao Island. And in February 2005, bombs exploded in three southern Philippine cities.

Scandal tainted Arroyo's presidency in 2005, when her opponents accused her of manipulating the 2004 presidential election results. She denied the accusations but admitted to a lapse in judgment for phoning an election official to discuss vote counting. In addition, members of her family have been accused of taking payoffs from illegal gambling. Although political opponents and public protests have called for her resignation, Arroyo has vowed to stay in office and continue her work toward economic and political progress in the Philippines.

Visit www.vgsbooks.com for links to websites with additional information about politics and government in the Philippines, including the latest information about Arroyo's controversial presidency.

Government

The constitution of 1987 provides for a bicameral (two-house) legislature. The senate contains twenty four members, who are elected on a nationwide basis to six-year terms. Senators must be at least thirty-five years of age and may serve no more than two consecutive terms. The house of representatives has two hundred members elected by districts for terms of three years. The president may appoint up to fifty additional representatives from among the nation's minority groups. Representatives must be at least twenty-five years old and can serve only three terms in a row.

The president directs the executive branch of government and is limited to one six-year term. Presidents must be at least forty years old when elected. The chief executive signs bills passed by the legislature and also acts as commander in chief. The president names the cabinet members, but they must be approved by the legislature's Commission of Appointments.

The Philippines's highest judicial body is the Supreme Court, which consists of a chief justice and fourteen associate justices. The president appoints these justices to terms of four years. The court of appeals has a presiding judge and thirty-five associate justices. Local courts exist in every city.

The republic is divided into thirteen regions, which are further broken down into seventy-three provinces. Councils guide the regions, and a governor and two provincial board members rule each province. All officials at the local levels are elected by their communities.

THE PEOPLE

About 83 million people live in the Philippines—more than ten times as many as in 1903, when census takers first surveyed the entire archipelago. About half of all Filipinos make their homes in the country's large cities. Nearly 40 percent of the total population lives in central Luzon, a region that includes the large urban area of Metro Manila.

The average population density in the Philippines is 722 people per square mile (279 per sq. km), compared to 79 people per square mile (31 per sq. km) in the United States. But much of the Philippines is mountainous, and many of its more than seven thousand islands are uninhabited. As a result, the population density varies widely from island to island. In the city of Manila, for example, the population density is 106,920 people per square mile (41,282 per sq. km), while the population density in the mountainous province of Apayao in central Luzon is only 62 people per square mile (24 per sq. km).

Ethnic Groups

The majority of Filipinos are descended from Malays. Waves of Malay immigrants settled in various regions of the country and over time developed into many distinct ethnic groups. In addition to the Malay immigrants, Aeta, Chinese, Arab, and Spanish people also made their way to the archipelago. Offspring from marriages between Chinese or Spanish people and Malays became known as mestizos. The name Filipinos—at first used to describe people born of Spanish parents on the islands—is a general name for all citizens of the country.

The Philippines contains more than eighty different ethnic groups. Many of these peoples, such as the descendants of the Aeta, live in remote parts of the islands. Their small communities have little contact with other villages. The Tagalog name for the many mountain-dwelling ethnic groups is Igorot, which means "mountaineer." The Bontoc and Ifugao are Malay-descended Igorots whose ancestors built the rice terraces on the mountainsides of northern Luzon.

THE MANGYAN

Made up of eight tribal groups, the Mangyan are the original inhabitants of Mindoro Island. Numbering about 100,000, they are farmers who live much as they have for centuries. Most Mangyan, who make their homes in the island's mountains, live in wood and thatch homes built on stilts. Each of the eight tribes has its own language and customs, including rich oral traditions of songs, folktales, and poetry.

A Mangyan girl carries a basket on her back. The Mangyan have preserved much of their traditional culture and view outsiders with suspicion. To learn more about the Philippines' indigenous populations, visit www.vgsbooks.com for links.

The Tagalogs are a lowland people who live on southern Luzon and on Mindoro. The most numerous of the ethnic groups on the islands, the Tagalogs make up more than one-quarter of the Filipino population. Because their regional home includes Manila, many Tagalogs play a highly visible role in Filipino politics and business.

The Ilocanos form another ethnic group of Malay ancestry, and for the most part they reside on the western coast of Luzon and in the Cagayan Valley. The Ilocanos have moved into prominence in Philippine life in part because Ferdinand Marcos—a member of the Ilocano—gave many of them government jobs during his presidency. The Pampangans, on the other hand, have been largely excluded from the national mainstream. Living mostly in the central plain, many Pampangans are members of the Huk movement and other revolutionary parties.

The ethnic groups of the Visayan Islands also use the name Visayan to describe their entire population. The Cebuano, Waray-Waray, and Ilongo are three of the ethnic subgroups that make up the Visayan people. Many of the groups in this region grow and process sugarcane.

Many Filipino Muslims live in the recently created ARMM, which has the fastest-growing population in the country. Other Muslims make their homes on the Sulu Archipelago. Filipino Muslims include the Maranao, Samal, and Yakan ethnic groups. In general, the Muslims form a religious minority in the Philippines, but they are the dominant faith in the areas that they occupy. In the ARMM, nine out of every ten residents are Muslim. The legal system, religious language (Arabic), and culture of the Muslims set them apart from the rest of the nation.

Languages

More than seventy-five languages and five hundred dialects are spoken throughout the Philippines. Most of them are part of the Malayo-Polynesian family of languages. Tagalog is used on western Luzon, and Ilocano is the main tongue on the northern part of the island. Cebuano is the chief language spoken by the ethnic groups on the Visayan Islands.

In an effort to establish a deeper sense of national unity, the government designated two official languages—Filipino and English. Most businesspeople, lawyers, government workers, doctors, and educators speak English. Its widespread use makes the Philippines one of the largest English-speaking countries in the world.

Filipino is based on Tagalog. In recent years, Filipinos have produced more radio programs, movies, and television shows in Filipino. This broad exposure to the language has created a growing population of Filipinos who speak Filipino. Spanish, which was widely spoken in the eighteenth and nineteenth centuries, is becoming rare.

A "Texting" Nation

The Philippines is a world leader in the use of text messaging, or texting. Rather than pay the high price of landline calls, Filipinos depend on their mobile phones for communication. Filipinos can be seen everywhere punching text messages into keypads. Those in their teens and twenties are so skilled with texting abbreviations that they are sometimes called Generation Text. Filipinos use texting to rally voters during elections or to bring out demonstrators to fight for social or political causes. Texting even shows up at office holiday parties. Employees hold competitions to see who is their company's texting champion.

Education

About 95 percent of Filipinos can read and write, although the literacy rate is greater among those in cities than it is in rural areas. The high literacy rate reflects the emphasis that Filipinos put on education. Public schools provide six years of elementary education to all Filipino children, and the law requires that children attend school from the ages of seven to twelve.

For many years, children received their schooling first in the language of the region and later in both Filipino and English. In 2003, however, President Arroyo ordered that instructors should use English as the language of education.

Students begin secondary school at the age of thirteen and continue for four years. They focus on general studies in the first two years and on either college preparatory or vocational courses in the second two years. About 80 percent of Filipinos who are aged thirteen to seventeen attend secondary classes.

The Philippines has many colleges and universities, located primarily in Manila. Students from all parts of Southeast Asia come to the islands to complete their educations. The University of the East, Santo Tomás University, Feati University, and the University of the Philippines are all within Metro Manila. These institutions offer a wide range of liberal arts and professional courses. Bicol University at Legazpi and Saint Louis University at Baguio are two of the post-secondary schools located outside of Manila.

Health

The physical health of Filipinos has improved significantly since the mid-1970s. By providing dietary information and food supplements, the government attacked the population's poor nutritional practices. As a result, mothers and their infants are in better health, and life expectancy figures have risen. In 2004 about 29 babies among every 1,000 newborns died within their first year of life. This figure is lower than the average rate of 41 per 1,000 in all of Southeast Asia. The Philippine life expectancy of 70 years also is better than the regional average of 68.

Great disparities exist between urban and rural Filipinos. The poverty rate in rural areas is nearly 50 percent, while the rate in the region around Manila is less than 15 percent. Recent studies show that residents of the national capital region earned nine times as much as those in the poorest regions of the country. And the richest 10 percent of the Philippine population had an income that was twenty-three times greater than the poorest 10 percent.

The Philippine government is striving to distribute health-care workers and facilities throughout the country. Of the 1,700 hospitals in the nation, about 25 percent are in central and southern Luzon. In the ARMM, one of the poorest regions of the country, there are about 15 hospitals. In an effort to provide basic health care to the country's rural population, the government has trained paramedics in disease control, sanitation, and nutrition. The government then stations these new medical

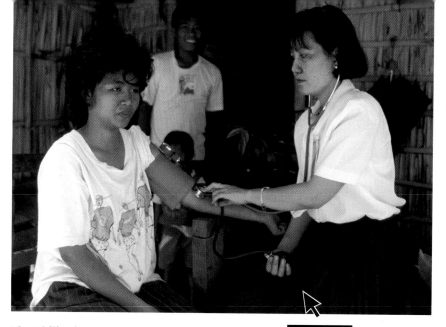

The Philippine government is striving to improve health-care in rural areas.

professionals in rural areas. Some hospitals in larger cities train doctors specifically to work in more remote regions of the country.

Among the principal illnesses that Filipino medical workers treat are malaria, pneumonia, intestinal diseases, and bronchitis. Doctors also care for people with HIV (human immunodeficiency virus) and AIDS (acquired immunodeficiency syndrome), diseases that weaken the immune system. By the early 2000s, about 9,500 adult Filipinos—or 0.1 percent—were living with HIV or AIDS. Health officials consider this figure low when compared to the rest of the world.

One cause of concern to those in charge of national health policies is the country's high population growth rate. Recent statistics show that the population has increased by about 2 percent each year. At that rate, the number of Filipinos will double in about thirty years. Religious beliefs that prohibit birth control and the Philippine tradition of large families make the population difficult to hold in check. High rates of population growth strain food resources, cause overcrowding in urban areas, and mean that more Filipinos will likely live in poverty.

High population growth rates strain the Philippine economy. Frustrated by the government's resistance to address the problem, Filipino business leaders are taking action. In 2004 they called for a national campaign on family planning and resolved to fund reproductive health services, which would include providing contraceptives. Business leaders believe reducing the population growth rate will spur economic growth, create more jobs, and reduce poverty.

CULTURAL LIFE

The Philippines is truly a mixed culture. Malay, Chinese, Spanish, Arab, and U.S. influences mingle with native traditions to create a rich cultural heritage. Also influenced by their religious beliefs and geographical location, Filipinos have developed a unique way of life that embraces the arts and celebrates their nation's history.

◉ Religion

More than 80 percent of Filipinos are Roman Catholic. Spanish missionaries brought Roman Catholicism to the islands in the sixteenth century. For several hundred years, only Spaniards could be members of the clergy. These days, however, most of the Catholic priests in the Philippines were born in the country.

At the turn of the twentieth century, Gregorio Aglipay began the Independent Philippine Church as an offshoot of the Roman Catholic Church. This church's membership is about 5 percent of the Filipino population. A distinctive feature of Aglipay's church is its focus on

Philippine patriotism, but this religious body also follows many Catholic doctrines. Other nationalistic Christian churches have grown up in recent decades, including the small but highly organized Iglesia ni Kristo. Members of this church number about 2 percent of the population.

Many Protestant sects developed roots in the Philippines beginning in the early 1900s. Small congregations of Episcopalians, Baptists, Lutherans, Methodists, and Presbyterians exist on the nation's principal islands. The Protestant groups—made up of about 5 percent of the population—have built and staffed many clinics and schools throughout the country.

Most followers of Islam—Muslims, who are often called Moros—live on Mindanao Island and in the Sulu Archipelago. The practices of Islam include praying five times each day, fasting during the holy month of Ramadan, donating to the poor and, if possible, traveling at least once to Mecca—the central city of Islam in

Saudi Arabia. The Quran—which records the visions received by Muhammad, the religion's founder—is the Islamic holy book. Muslims in the Philippines often feel greater bonds with Muslims in Malaysia and in the rest of the Islamic world than they do with the Christian population in their own country. About 5 percent of all Filipinos are followers of Islam.

Holidays and Celebrations

Religious holidays are a big part of life in the Philippines. In the days leading up to Christmas, Catholic priests organize processions either early in the morning or late at night. As they walk, villagers sing and carry lanterns, banners, and flowers. The city of San Fernando on Luzon hosts a spectacular lantern festival, featuring a parade of giant lanterns that are each 40 feet (12 m) in diameter and hold thousands of twinkling lights. From Christmas Eve to New Year's Day, the boom of firecrackers echoes across the islands. On Christmas Day, many residents sit down to a traditional dinner of roast pig.

Easter is the most important religious holiday for the nation's Christians. Called *Cuaresma* or *Semana Santa* in the Philippines, the Holy Week leading up to Easter starts with Palm Sunday. Catholics carry palm leaves, or *palaspas*, to church for the priest to bless. On Maundy Thursday (Holy Thursday), Catholics attend passion plays, which relate the sufferings of Jesus. Good Friday is a somber day on which many believers attend reenactments of the death of Jesus. Catholic churches keep their doors open all through

Children carry a float bearing a statue of the crucified Jesus during an **Easter procession.**

the night for the faithful to pray. Some Catholics try to visit as many churches as they can in a practice known as *visita iglesia*. At dawn on Easter Sunday, during a procession called the *Salubong*, villagers carry statues of Jesus and his mother, Mary, to the church. This tradition commemorates the encounter between Mary and her son after his death. Easter Sunday is a day of joyful celebration in churches and villages throughout the country.

Every year in mid-December, the Philippines' Muslim population remembers the arrival of Islam in the region. In the 1300s, Shariff Kabungsuan landed at the mouth of the Rio Grande at Cotabato on Mindanao, bringing the Muslim faith to the local inhabitants. During the Shariff Kabungsuan Festival, residents of Cotabato reenact the arrival, attend musical and sporting events, and hold boat races.

Nearly every city and village in the Philippines holds at least one fiesta—or festival—each year. Most of these occasions celebrate community life and honor the feast day of the town's patron saint. Young people who have moved away from their families often return home for the annual fiesta.

One of the largest fiestas is the Ati-Atihan Festival in Kalibo on the Visayan island of Panay. Taking place every January, this celebration honors Santo Niño, Kalibo's patron saint. It also commemorates a thirteenth-century land deal between the Ati king, Marikudo, and ten chieftains who had migrated north from Borneo. To the heavy beat of

ALL SAINTS' DAY

Every year on November 1, Catholic Filipino families gather at gravesites to remember their relatives who have passed away. Known as All Saints' Day, or All Souls' Day, it is an occasion for both respect and celebration. Some families sleep in the cemetery the night before, then paint the grave, arrange flowers, light candles, and pray the next day. Later, the festivities begin. Families feast and listen to music, sometimes celebrating in the cemetery until late into the night.

A family keeps vigil at a relative's grave on All Saint's Day.

Costumed dancers participate in the **Ati-Atihan Festival,** a weeklong celebration in Kalibo. The name of the Philippines' most famous festival means "making like Ati." The Ati were the original inhabitants of Panay Island.

drums, thousands of brightly costumed revelers dance and celebrate from sunrise to sunset during this weeklong fiesta. The event ends with a grand procession through the streets. This festival is so popular that many other communities in the Visayas have created their own Ati-Atihan fiestas.

National holidays include Independence Day on June 12, the date in 1898 when the Philippines declared the country free of foreign rule. National Heroes Day is the last Sunday in August. Rizal Day on December 30 honors José Rizal, the country's national hero. Thousands of Filipinos gather every year on this date in Manila's Rizal Park for a remembrance ceremony.

Music and Dance

Music has long played an important role in lives of Filipinos. The native music of the Philippines varies from region to region. On southern islands, *kulintang* music features gongs and other percussion instruments. In the lighthearted *sindil* style, singers trade jokes in song backed by the music of a xylophone and a *biyula*, a traditional violin. Native musicians in the north accompany dance performances on gongs called *gansa*, as well as a variety of drums. Other native instruments include a bamboo zither and the *kutiyapi*, a type of lute.

With themes of love, fate, and death, the *kundiman* genre of music has long been popular among Filipinos. The lyrics of these emotional melodies usually address romantic themes such as sacrifice for love or the broken-hearted regret over the loss of love. With origins in the early 1800s, these songs are still popular with modern artists, who often combine current musical trends with traditional folk music.

In the late 1950s, Filipinos wrote lyrics to American rock songs in their native Tagalog language, resulting in the birth of Pinoy (or Filipino) rock. Many Filipino musicians made the rock-and-roll genre their own by mixing it with traditional folk music. In the 1980s, Pinoy rock mixed with other genres such as reggae or punk rock, and Pinoy rock became the music of protesters as thousands of Filipinos demonstrated against President Ferdinand Marcos's regime. In the early 2000s, hip-hop and rhythm and blues dominated the music scene.

The Philippines has a long tradition of dance. Filipino ethnic dances often draw their themes from the world of nature. The country's national folk dance is the *tinikling*, which mimics a heron hopping through rice fields. In this dance, two people hold bamboo poles just above the ground and strike them together as a

A **Filipino rock group** performs at a club in Manila.

boy and girl hop between them in time to the music. Another version of this dance often performed in the Muslim community is the *singkil*, in which two dancers jump among four poles struck at increasing speed.

Many Filipinos in urban areas have a passion for ballet. The National Ballet Federation sponsors Filipinos as they study and perform classical ballet. Performances often mix classical ballet with Philippine folktales and traditional music. Modern dance—a style that emphasizes natural, flowing movement—also holds a prominent place in the nation's cultural life.

◐ Visual Arts and Literature

Many visual artists have worked in the Philippines since the early 1800s, when Spanish influence was especially strong. The painter Felix Resureccion Hidalgo is the most famous Filipino artist of the colonial period. Juan Luna, another colonial-era painter, employed a realistic style and also gained international fame. Painters Fabian de la Rosa and Fernando Amorsolo dominated the first half of the twentieth century. De la Rosa was known for his portrait work, while Amorsolo gained fame for the free-flowing brushstrokes of his landscapes. In the mid-1900s, José Joya earned praise as a pioneer in modern Philippine abstract art. Sculptor Guillermo Tolentino, who was named a National Artist in 1973, is famous for his classical artwork. Many museums and galleries in the Philippines encourage young artists by providing space for them to show their work.

Philippine actors appear on both stage and screen. Theaters throughout the country draw large audiences with world-famous plays and big-scale musicals, as well as smaller stage productions penned by local writers. Since the early twentieth century, many filmmakers have worked in the Philippines, producing popular movies in English and Filipino. Action movies and romantic comedies are favorites for moviegoers. Followers of serious Philippine cinema seek out works by Lino Brocka and Ishmael

SOAP OPERA BUFFS

Soap operas, or *teleseryes*, dominate evening television programming in the Philippines. Some of the country's most famous and most talented actors star in these tales of love, intrigue, and revenge. Fans love to escape into the tangled story lines. But many observers think soap operas communicate the wrong values and are harmful to Philippine culture and family life.

Bernal. These directors, who both worked in the 1970s and 1980s, used their art to send a social message. Brocka's films reflect the lives of the poor, while Bernal's work deals with the Filipino struggle against oppression.

Philippine architecture varies widely and reflects historic events and foreign rule. Simple huts made of bamboo poles and nipa leaves represent native architecture. Spanish influence appears in buildings constructed of adobe (clay) blocks. In the 1930s, many architects turned to the modern art deco style, which featured clean lines and geometric shapes. After World War II bombings destroyed much of Manila, a mixture of styles emerged as the city was rebuilt. Several massive concrete buildings designed by 1970s architect Leandro Locsin stand in Manila. In recent years, sleek skyscrapers dominate the skylines of major Philippine cities.

Philippine literature began as folktales and poems passed from generation to generation in the oral tradition—a practice that continues in modern times. At the close of the nineteenth century, José Rizal, the

The Jai Alai building, once one of the Philippines' finest art deco buildings, was demolished in 2000. The Philippines struggles to preserve its architectural past while meeting the demands of continued growth in large cities such as Manila.

Farewell, my
adored Land, region of
the sun caressed,
Pearl of the Orient Sea, our
Eden lost,
With gladness I give you my Life,
sad and repressed;
And were it more brilliant, more
fresh and at its best,
I would still give it to you for
your welfare at most.

—from José Rizal's poem,
Mi Último Adiós, 1896

Philippine independence leader, wrote a novel that has become a national classic, *Noli Me Tangere (Touch Me Not)*. Originally written in Spanish, Rizal's powerful stories focus on the Filipino search for self-rule. He wrote what many consider his master-piece, *Mi Ultimo Adios (My Last Farewell)*, in 1896, on the eve of his execution. Other influential Philippine writers include the poets Francisco Balagtas and José Garcia Villa, and modern novelist and playwright Nick Joaquin.

Sports and Recreation

Traditional sports in the Philippines include *arnis*—a form of sword combat that uses wooden sticks—and *sipa*, which resembles volley-ball. Many Filipinos enjoy basketball, which is often considered the national sport. Players compete on organized teams in schools and at the professional level. Baseball and jai alai, or *pelota*—a high-speed game played on a long, open-air court—are other major sports. Many Filipinos also enjoy billiards, golf, and ten-pin bowling.

Basketball is one of the most popular sports in the Philippines. Here young boys play a pickup game in a field.

The winners of the **Binibining Pilipinas 2005** wave after being crowned. The three women will represent the Philippines in the Miss Universe, Miss World, and Miss International beauty pageants.

Chess is another popular pastime. Filipinos of many ages hold chess matches in both urban and rural areas. The Philippines has supplied several grand masters (champions) to the international chess tour.

Tupada (gamecock fights) occur in most of the villages, towns, and cities of the country. Competitors put their roosters—which are fitted with sharp blades behind one leg—into a pit to do battle until one of the animals wounds the other. A centuries-old spectator sport, tupada is a popular recreation that continues to entertain many Filipinos.

Food

Filipino food combines Malay, Chinese, Arab, and Spanish influences. Rice and seafood are the main ingredients in daily fare. Seafood from the

BEAUTY PAGEANTS

Beauty pageants are a big part of the Filipino culture. Nearly every city, town, and small village across the country holds an annual beauty pageant. Because many young Filipinas cannot afford college, they see beauty pageants as a way to jumpstart their careers. Winning the nation's biggest pageant—the annual Binibining Pilipinas—leads to advertising contracts and the possibility of television and film work. This enthusiasm for beauty pageants has led to international success. The Philippines became the first Asian country to win five major international beauty pageant crowns—two for Miss Universe and three for Miss International.

nation's coastal waters is often cooked over coals or prepared raw in a tangy sauce called *kilawin*. Filipino fish soup—*sinigang*—is often made from a base of tamarind (a tropical fruit) that has a tangy, sour taste.

Among the best-known Filipino dishes is *adobo*, a Spanish-style stew made from chicken and pork and cooked with vinegar and garlic. The dish's Chinese influence is evident in its use of soy sauce. Another distinctive Filipino food is *lechon* (roasted pork), which is served at festivals. During national holidays and at large family gatherings, cooks roast a whole pig by turning it slowly over coals. Other typical Filipino foods include pasta noodles called *pancit*, and eggrolls called *lumpia*, which cooks make from pork and cabbage.

HALO-HALO

Halo-halo, which means "mix-mix," is a cool, creamy Filipino snack that is especially popular in the hot summer months. Cooks use a variety of sweet flavors, depending on their personal taste and the fruits that are in season. Here is one version of this favorite Filipino dish.

½ cup canned sweet corn or chickpeas (garbanzo beans)

1 cup cooked sweet potatoes, cut into ½-inch cubes

1 large ripe banana, cut into ½-inch slices

1 cup shredded cantaloupe or honeydew melon

2 ripe mangoes or 1 cup canned mango, cut into ½-inch cubes

1 cup shredded coconut, fresh or canned

1 cup flavored gelatin, cut into ½-inch cubes

2 cups shaved ice

2 cups milk

4 scoops of your favorite ice cream

½ cup chopped peanuts or toasted rice cereal

1. Layer the first eight ingredients in four tall glasses. Put one-fourth of each ingredient in each glass in the order listed. Start with the sweet corn or chickpeas on the bottom and put shaved ice on the top.
2. Pour ½ cup milk into each glass.
3. Top each glass with a scoop of ice cream.
4. Sprinkle nuts or toasted rice cereal on the ice cream.

Serves 4

Halo-halo is a popular Filipino treat.

Filipinos use coconuts to make soups and to brew an alcoholic beverage called *lambanog*. Coconut milk—an ingredient that reflects Malay influence—is used to flavor meats and vegetables. Common Filipino fruits include mangoes, bananas, rambutans (red, oval-shaped fruit), watermelons, and papayas. Cooks of the islands often mix a number of fruits together into a delicious snack called *halo-halo*.

To learn more about Filipino cultural life, visit www.vgsbooks.com. There you'll find links to information on Ethiopia's many traditions, including music, religion, holidays and festivals, sports, food and recipes, and more.

THE ECONOMY

After suffering many years of decline during the Marcos regime, the Philippine economy began to rebound in the late 1980s under new leadership. The country stayed on a path toward economic stability despite several factors that threatened growth in the early 1990s. Oil prices soared, raising energy costs. And natural disasters—including an earthquake in central Luzon and the eruption of Mount Pinatubo—required funds for cleanup and rebuilding. In the mid-1990s, under President Ramos, the government introduced a wide range of economic reforms that spurred the rapid growth of businesses and foreign investment.

In 1997 a financial crisis hit many Asian countries. The value of currency in these countries fell, causing economic hardship. Although the Philippine economy suffered a slump, it was not as severely affected as its neighbors, partly because of the government's more conservative economic policies. By 1999 the country's economy showed signs of recovery, and in recent years, President

Arroyo's administration has pushed the country toward more rapid economic growth. In 2004 the gross domestic product, or GDP (the value of goods and services produced annually in a country), increased to a strong 6.1 percent.

Service Sector

Service industries—which include government, education, trade, transportation, finance, tourism, and communication—are the largest contributor to the GDP at 53 percent. About 48 percent of all Filipinos work in the service sector. The government considers trade, transportation, and communications its most important services.

The Philippines' major trading partners are Asian neighbors—Japan, Singapore, South Korea, China, Taiwan, and Malaysia—and the United States. The value of the Philippines' imports is about equal to the value of its exports. Chemicals, machinery, and petroleum are

 Jeepneys **are the most common form of taxi service in the Philippines. The first jeepneys were U.S. Army jeeps left over from World War II.**

major imports. Electronics and clothing are the country's most valuable exports. The Philippines also exports bananas, coconut products, gold, copper, pineapples, and sugar.

The mountainous terrain of the Philippines makes transportation difficult, but the government is working to establish a network of highways and ferries to ease movement throughout the islands. The Philippines has more than 125,000 miles (200,000 km) of roads, of which about 20 percent are paved. Because few Filipinos own cars, jeepneys—brightly painted taxis—serve local transportation needs. The Philippine National Railway has more than 500 miles (900 km) of train track, most of which is on Luzon. A rapid transit system knits Metro Manila together by rail. Boat and airplane routes link the many islands of the Philippines. Manila, Cebu, and Davao are among the major interisland ports for freighters that carry goods and for ferryboats that transport people. Small aircraft connect the islands, with Philippine Airlines serving as the nation's principal domestic and international carrier. Manila Airport is a hub for air traffic from all over the world.

Communications is a big business in the Philippines. Nearly half of all Filipinos own cell phones, and they send more than 200 million text messages each day. In late 2004,

Text messaging

the government began work on bringing the newest digital communications technology—systems currently used in the United States and Europe—to the archipelago. About 5 million Filipinos have access to the Internet, a low figure compared to neighboring Asian nations. The Philippines has about twenty major newspapers, the largest of which are the *Manila Bulletin* and the *Manila Times*. Several television networks broadcast across the islands. In urban areas, about two-thirds of all households have televisions. One-half of all households in rural areas have televisions.

Industry

Most of the industries of the Philippines are located in or near Manila. Smaller factories process sugarcane, coconuts, tobacco, abaca, and latex from rubber trees. Other manufacturers produce textiles, paper products, electronics, furniture, and medicinal drugs. Filipinos also work in heavy industry, making cement, fertilizers, chemicals, steel, and glass. About 16 percent of the Filipino labor pool is employed in industrial plants, which provide about 32 percent of the GDP.

After growing steadily since the 1950s, profits from manufacturing fell each year in the early 1980s. In 1986 the government sold many of the companies that Marcos had nationalized (put under state ownership), returning more than one hundred businesses to the private sphere. Recent administrations have encouraged foreign and domestic investment by offering tax breaks and generous credit terms.

The Philippines continues to import more manufactured goods—especially heavy machinery—than it produces. Textiles and electronics are among the nation's major exports. The government has encouraged the development of new industries, especially on sites away from Manila. In recent years, the government has worked to improve transportation and communication in areas outside the capital city, hoping that new industries will take root there and raise money for the country's treasury.

REMITTANCES

An average of 2,500 Filipinos leave their country every day to work abroad, making the Philippines one of the largest exporters of labor in the world. An estimated 10 percent of the country's population—about 8 million people—work in more than 180 countries around the world. The money they send home to their families—called remittances—contributes greatly to the Philippine economy. In 2003 alone, Filipinos working abroad sent home $7.6 billion.

59

Agriculture, Fishing, and Forestry

An estimated 36 percent of the Filipino workforce is involved in agriculture, fishing, and forestry, and these workers produce more than 15 percent of the nation's GDP. Farms in the Philippines range from small, rented plots to large, mechanized plantations. Most farming families own or rent their fields. Attempts at land reform allowed more Filipinos to hold property, but much of the nation's land still belongs to a relatively small group of landowners.

Farmers cultivate about 25 percent of the country, and of that area, about two-thirds is used to raise rice and corn. The irrigated farms of central Luzon grow high-yield rice crops, as do the Cagayan Valley and the western Visayan Islands. Improved farming methods and the use of hybrid seeds have helped increase rice production. Only a few years ago, the Philippines imported rice. These days they meet their own needs. Other food crops include sweet potatoes and cassavas (starchy root crops).

Filipino farmers cultivate some crops—including bananas, pineapples, mangoes, and coconuts—both for local demand and for export. About 3.5 million farmers grow coconuts in the country's coastal areas, giving the Philippines a 60 percent share in the world's export of coconuts. Workers process coconuts into copra—dried coconut meat—or into oil. About 25 million Filipinos make their living solely from the coconut industry. Sugarcane, another major export crop, thrives on western and northeastern Negros Island and on central Luzon. Abaca plants provide fiber from which workers make a strong rope known as Manila hemp. Plantations and small farms alike cultivate rubber and tobacco crops that are sold abroad.

With many miles of coastline and with most of its population living near the sea, the Philippines has long

CYANIDE FISHING

The Philippines provides about 80 percent of the world's live tropical aquarium fish. Fishers catch the fish in the country's coral reef areas, where there is a great diversity of species. An estimated 70 to 90 percent of the fish are caught using a method known as cyanide fishing. Divers squirt a solution of the chemical cyanide into areas where fish are hiding, stunning them so that they can be easily gathered. The cyanide kills some of the fish, either immediately or during their journey to market. The cyanide not only affects the fish but also does great damage to coral reefs. Although the Philippine government has outlawed cyanide fishing, the practice still continues.

been a fishing nation. Filipinos eat freshly caught fish at many of their meals. Refrigeration and processing plants enable them to store and transport fish products safely. The islands lie within an ocean area that is rich in both its variety and quantity of seafood. Bonitos, shrimp, crabs, tuna, mackerel, anchovies, sardines, and swordfish are some of the species taken from Philippine waters. In the Sulu Archipelago, fishers find large numbers of mollusks, which yield mother-of-pearl (a hard, pearly material) from the inner layer of their shells. This substance is often used in Filipino jewelry. Milkfish, tilapia, and shrimp grow in ponds that Filipinos have set up at the mouths of rivers and along the coasts.

Motorized trawlers, which drag huge nets behind them, make up over half of the commercial fishing fleet in the Philippines. Many Filipino fishers, however, still use the traditional *bancas*—wooden-hulled fishing boats with outriggers (frames) that project from the side for stability. Crews on these boats cast lines or throw single nets by hand.

Forests cover about one-fourth of the Philippines. More than three thousand varieties of trees grow on the islands, but most of the lumber that is cut down for export is Philippine mahogany. Mangrove trees from the coastal areas are also an important

Filipino fishers set sail in traditional **bancas.**

When dried, the hollow, woody stem of **bamboo** has many valuable uses. It can be used to fashion flooring, siding, fencing, furniture, boats, tools, animal cages, baskets, and much more. To learn more about bamboo, visit www.vgsbooks.com for links.

commercial timber. Pine forests that thrive at high elevations, especially on Luzon and Mindoro, provide another lumber source. Ceiba trees yield kapok, a fiber that is used as stuffing in some mattresses and life preservers. Bamboo plants grow in groves throughout the islands. Construction workers use bamboo to build homes in rural areas, and craftspeople use it to make mats, baskets, and other items.

Energy and Mining

To fuel vehicles and to provide energy for domestic and industrial use, the Philippines imports large quantities of petroleum. Deep-sea oil reserves off the coast of Palawan supply less than 10 percent of the nation's energy needs. To encourage development of energy resources, the government began offering incentives to foreign investors, and by 2004 more than sixty international companies had entered the Philippine oil industry.

In an effort to reduce the nation's dependence on oil, the government has made expanding natural gas use a major goal. The discovery of a large natural gas field off the shores of Palawan Island in 1992 led to the largest natural gas development project in Philippine history. By 2001 a 312-mile (504 km) pipeline—one of

This **geothermal power plant** is located on the island of Leyte. Unlike many other sources of power, geothermal power is not harmful to the environment because it does not produce any toxic gases or other harmful substances.

the longest deep-water pipelines in the world—linked the gas fields to three power stations in Batangas, in southern Luzon. Future plans call for the construction of an additional pipeline to Metro Manila.

Hydroelectricity and geothermal power (heat from within the earth) are two of the nation's most promising energy sources. Hydroelectricity generates about 15 percent of the country's power. Construction recently began on two major hydropower projects on Luzon. More than 20 percent of the Philippines' electricity comes from geothermal power. The government plans to construct several more geothermal plants in the coming years. The Philippines is second only to the United States in its use of geothermal power. The government is also studying the country's potential to generate solar (sun) power and wind power.

The Philippines has large reserves of several minerals. Its copper, nickel, and chromite supplies are among the largest in the world. Miners have found gold on northern Luzon and in the mountains of Mindanao. Coal, iron ore, limestone, zinc, and silver are also mined in the islands. The mining industry began declining in the late

With about 250 operations, the Philippine jewelry industry employs about 100,000 goldsmiths, stone setters, and other workers. But with the country's ready supplies of gold and silver, many observers believe the industry is underdeveloped. Among them is the government, which is actively working to draw investors.

Clark Air Base, before the U.S. military left in 1991. Visit www.vgsbooks.com for links to more information about the Clark Special Economic Zone.

THE CLARK SPECIAL ECONOMIC ZONE

Once the largest U.S. military base outside the continental United States, Clark Air Base has become the Clark Special Economic Zone. The U.S. military left the base in 1991, when the eruption of Mount Pinatubo buried it in ash. Since that time, the Philippine government has cleaned up volcanic debris and has ambitious plans for development, including industry and tourist attractions. Located in central Luzon, Clark is also the future home of a state-of-the-art international airport. High-speed trains will carry passengers and cargo between the airport and Manila to the south.

1980s, due to low metal prices and high production costs. A Philippine Supreme Court decision in 2004 prohibits foreign companies from full ownership of mining operations. This ruling has discouraged some international investment in the Philippine mining industry.

◉ The Future

After many years of martial law under Ferdinand Marcos, democracy seems to have taken hold in the Philippines. Considerable progress toward cleaning up corruption in government has been made, but scandals still emerge. President Arroyo must work to overcome recent allegations of fixing election results in order to assure the country's political stability. Her administration also must deal with continued threats from militant Muslim separatist groups, particularly the terrorist organization Abu Sayyaf. Working with the United States, Arroyo has vowed to defeat Abu Sayyaf and protect the Philippines from terrorism.

Under Arroyo, the Philippine government has made great strides toward economic stability. Still, nearly 40 percent of the population lives in poverty, and the income disparity between the richest and poorest households is growing. A focus on economic growth in cities has made conditions especially difficult in rural areas, where there are few job opportunities and low wages. Improving the way of life for all Filipinos will continue to challenge the government in the coming years.

"This nation is at a crossroads: quite simply, it must reform or perish."

—President Gloria Arroyo

An even greater challenge may be unchecked population growth. The government has not established plans to reduce the rising birthrate. Many experts believe that countrywide action is needed to limit population growth. Until such action is taken, overcrowding, food and energy shortages, strains on health and education resources, and a lack of jobs will most likely threaten the nation's progress.

Timeline

CA. 25,000 B.C. The Aeta people arrive in the Philippines.

3,000 B.C. Early inhabitants create the Angono Petroglyphs in southern Luzon.

1500–500 B.C. Malays and people from China and Vietnam begin settling in the Philippines.

A.D. 600s–1100s Sri Vijayans control trade and sea routes in the Philippines.

1200s Majapahit rulers from Java take control of Philippine sea trade and introduce Hinduism.

1300s Arab scholars introduce Islam to the southern islands. Chinese merchants establish settlements on Luzon.

1500s Muslims clash with Chinese settlers and extend their influence north throughout much of Luzon.

1521 Explorer Ferdinand Magellan arrives in the Philippines under the Spanish flag and is killed by Lapu-Lapu warriors on Mactan.

1545 Spanish explorer Ruy Lopez de Villalobos names the Philippines after King Phillip II of Spain.

1565 Miguel Lopez de Legazpi founds the first Spanish colony on Cebu Island. Catholic missionaries spread Christianity to the Philippines.

1571 Spanish troops defeat the Moros and battle the Igorots.

1762 Filipino leader Diego Silang rebels against Spanish officials and establishes a government in Vigan.

1800s The Spanish open the Philippines to European trade.

1807 The Ilocanos on Luzon revolt against the Spanish.

1841 Apolonario de la Cruz leads a revolt against Spanish oppression.

1891 José Rizal establishes the Filipino League.

1892 Andres Bonifacio founds the Katipunan.

1898 U.S. and Katipunan forces defeat the Spanish in the Spanish-American War. Katipunan leader Emilio Aguinaldo declares independence for the Philippines, which is rejected by the United States.

1908 The University of the Philippines opens with funding from U.S. citizens.

1935 The United States gives Filipinos internal control of their country. Manuel Luis Quezon y Molina is elected president.

1941   Japanese troops invade the Philippines. The United States
        and the Philippines enter World War II.

1942   The Philippines surrenders to Japan.

1945   Japan surrenders to the United States, officially ending World War II.

1946   The United States withdraws from the Philippines, and the country gains
        full independence. The Huk Rebellion begins.

1953   Ramón Magsaysay is elected president and halts the Huk Rebellion.

1961   Diosdado Macapagal is elected president.

1965   Ferdinand Marcos is elected president.

1969   Extremist Muslim groups on Mindanao forms the Moro National Liberation Front
        (MNLF) to fight for self-rule of the southern islands.

1972   Marcos declares martial law when demonstrators create unrest.

1973   A new constitution gives Marcos control of the Philippines and an unlimited term in
        office.

1981   Under pressure from the Roman Catholic Church, Marcos ends martial law.

1983   Marcos opposition leader Benigno Aquino is assassinated in Manila.

1986   Under international pressure, Marcos steps down and flees to Hawaii. Corazon Aquino
        becomes president.

1987   Filipino voters approve a new constitution.

1991   Mount Pinatubo erupts on Luzon. U.S. military withdraws from all its bases in the
        Philippines.

1992   Filipinos elect as president Fidel Ramos, who signs a peace agreement with the MNLF
        that creates a region of self-rule for Muslims. Large oil and natural gas reserves
        are discovered off the coast of Palawan.

1997   The Asian financial crisis affects the value of currency in the region.

2001   President Joseph Estrada resigns under charges of corruption. Gloria
        Macapagal-Arroyo becomes president.

2004   The terrorist group Abu Sayyaf bombs a Philippine passenger ferry, killing
        more than one hundred people. Arroyo wins the presidential election.

2005   President Arroyo is accused of rigging 2004 presidential election
        results.

COUNTRY NAME Republic of the Philippines

AREA 115,830 square miles (300,000 sq. km)

MAIN LANDFORMS Sierra Madre, Cagayan Valley, Cordillera Central, Caraballo Mountains, Zambales Mountains, Mount Mayon, Mount Canlaon, Mount Nangtud, Iloilo Plain, Diuata Mountains, Agusan River valley, Katanglad Mountains, Mount Apo, Cotabato Valley, Zamboanga Mountains

HIGHEST POINT Mount Apo, 9,692 feet (2,954 m) above sea level

MAJOR RIVERS Cagayan, Pampanga, Agno, Agusan, Mindanao

ANIMALS Carabao, geckos, monitor lizards, monkeys, mouse deer, parrots, Philippine eagles, pythons, tamarau, tarsiers

CAPITAL CITY Manila

OTHER MAJOR CITIES Quezon City, Davao, Cebu City, Iloilo

OFFICIAL LANGUAGES Filipino and English

MONETARY UNIT Philippine peso. 1 peso = 100 centavos.

FILIPINO CURRENCY

The Philippines' official currency is the peso. The name *peso* comes from the Latin word *pensum*, meaning "weight." The country's smallest bill in circulation is 20 pesos, and the largest is 1,000 pesos. The front side of each bill features important people in Philippine history.

The reverse side shows landmarks and events in the country's history. The Philippines issues a variety of coins, ranging from 1 centavo to 10 pesos. A few coins feature prominent Filipinos, but most are simply stamped with the coin's denomination.

Currency Fast Facts

Adopted in 1898, the flag of the Philippines features three main colors. Blue stands for noble ideals, red represents courage, and white symbolizes peace. The flag has two horizontal bands—one red and one blue—and a white triangle. In the center of the triangle is a yellow sun, which stands for freedom and justice. The sun has eight rays, one for each province that revolted against Spanish rule. The three stars surrounding the sun represent the three main parts of the country—Luzon, the Visayas, and Mindanao.

Adopted in 1956 and confirmed by law in 1998, the national anthem of the Philippines is "Lupang Hinirang," or "Beloved Land." Music teacher Julian Felipe composed the music in 1898. The lyrics, taken from a poem written in Spanish by a soldier named José Palma, were added the following year. During the 1900s, translators created versions in both English and Filipino, but a national symbols law passed in 1998 declared that the anthem should be sung in Filipino. An English translation of the first two verses follows.

Lupang Hinirang (Beloved Land)
Land of the morning
Child of the sun returning
With fervor burning
Thee do our souls adore.

Land dear and holy,
Cradle of noble heroes,
Ne'er shall invaders
Trample thy sacred shores.

For a link to a website where you can listen to the Filipino national anthem, "Lupang Hinirang" (Beloved Land), visit www.vgsbooks.com.

LEVI CELERIO (1910–2002) Born in the Tondo neighborhood of Manila, Celerio started taking violin lessons at the age of eleven and earned a scholarship to Manila's Academy of Music. He became the youngest member of the Manila Symphony Orchestra, but his career as a violinist was cut short after he fell from a tree and broke his wrist. In 1930 Celerio's long career as a composer and lyricist began when he was asked to create the first of many theme songs for a movie. His songs eventually earned him a Lifetime Achievement Award from the Film Academy of the Philippines. In all, Celerio wrote four thousand songs. Named a National Artist for Music and Literature in 1997, Celerio also translated or wrote new lyrics to many traditional Filipino songs.

NICK JOAQUIN (1917–2004) A novelist, playwright, poet, journalist, and biographer, Joaquin was born in the Paco district of Manila. He was one of the Philippines's most accomplished writers. Starting as a proofreader for the *Free Press* (Philippines) in 1950, Joaquin rose through the ranks to become a literary editor and essayist under the name Quijano de Manila. He often wrote about the Philippines's history and cultural heritage. Proclaimed a National Novelist in 1976, Joaquin's numerous works include the short story "Summer Solstice," the novels *The Woman Who Had Two Navels* and *Cave and Shadows*, and the play *A Portrait of the Artist as Filipino*.

FE DEL MUNDO (b. 1911) An internationally known pediatrician, del Mundo's career as a researcher, teacher, hospital administrator, and humanitarian spans several decades. Born in Intramuros in Manila, she was the first Asian woman admitted to Harvard Medical School. Del Mundo went on to invent a low-cost incubator for premature babies. She also developed a device to relieve a condition called jaundice in babies. Named a National Scientist of the Philippines, del Mundo founded the Fe del Mundo Medical Center in Quezon City. This pediatric teaching hospital trains doctors to serve in rural and remote communities.

RAFAEL "PAENG" NEPOMUCENO (b. 1957) Born in Manila, Paeng was named the Filipino Athlete of the Century in 1999. He is widely known as the greatest bowler in the history of the sport. He is a six-time world champion and the only bowler to win the World Cup four times. Considered a national sports hero, Paeng received the Legion of Honor medal, the highest award given to a Filipino citizen.

FERNANDO POE JR. (1939–2004) Also known as FPJ and Da King, Poe was born in Manila. He was a popular and award-winning actor who made more than two hundred films during his fifty-year career. He often played characters who stood up for the poor and the downtrodden. Poe also directed nine movies and created a successful film production company. In 2003 he made an unsuccessful bid for the presidency, promising to solve the problems of the working poor in the Philippines.

CARLOS P. ROMULO (1899–1985) Romulo was born in Manila. As a journalist, Romulo won the Pulitzer Prize for Peace for his pre-World War II articles about the military situation in the Pacific. Romulo later became the Philippines's secretary of information. He served as president of the United Nations General Assembly from 1949 to 1950, when he became secretary for foreign affairs for the Philippines. Romulo was named the Philippine ambassador to the United States in 1952 and served in several other government posts. His autobiography, *I Walked with Heroes*, was published in 1961.

JENNIFER ROSALES (b. 1978) Born in Manila, Rosales started playing golf with her family when she was twelve years old and went on to become a five-time champion of the Philippine Ladies Amateur Open. She turned professional in 2000 after finding success on the University of Southern California golf team. In 2004 Rosales became the first player from the Philippines to win on the Ladies Professional Golf Association Tour. That same year, she had five top-ten finishes and placed fourth at the U.S. Women's Open.

LEA SALONGA (b. 1971) A singer and actress, Salonga was born in Manila. She appeared in her first stage production at the age of seven and later hosted her own show on Filipino television. She made a hit record, *Small Voice*, when she was ten years old. In London in 1989 and later on Broadway in New York, Salonga took on the role of Kim in the musical *Miss Saigon*, earning a Tony Award for her performance. She was also the singing voice for two Disney characters—Jasmine in the movie *Aladdin* and the title character in *Mulan*.

JAIME SIN (1928–2005) Born in New Washington in Aklan Province in the Visayas, Sin was ordained as a Catholic priest in 1954. He became the archbishop of Manila in 1972. In 1976 Pope Paul VI elevated Sin to cardinal, a position he held until his death. Sin became known to all Filipinos as a leader of the People Power Movement, which worked to unseat President Ferdinand Marcos and his oppressive regime in 1986. Sin again became the spiritual leader of a reborn People Power Movement in 1991 to help oust corrupt president Joseph Estrada.

GUILLERMO TOLENTINO (1890–1976) One of the greatest Filipino sculptors, Tolentino is famous for his masterpiece, the Bonifacio Monument in Caloocan City. This bronze sculpture shows the first encounter between Spanish soldiers and national hero Andres Bonifacio's revolutionary group, Katipunan, in 1896. Completed in 1933, Tolentino's intricate work stands as a national symbol of freedom and hope. In 1973 the Philippines government named Tolentino a National Artist for Sculpture.

APO REEF MARINE NATURAL PARK Apo Reef in the Visayas covers an area of about 200 square miles (520 sq. km) and is made up of most of the 450 species of coral that live in Philippine waters. In a few places, the coral juts above the surface of the water to create small islands, the largest of which is Apo. The park has become a favorite destination for snorkelers and scuba divers, who regularly encounter sharks, barracuda, sea turtles, and tuna. Divers also see smaller fish, such as angelfish, batfish, and surgeonfish, swimming among live corals, which include gorgonian sea fans and brain coral.

BANAUE RICE TERRACES About two thousand years ago, the Ifugao people carved rice terraces into the rugged mountains of northern Luzon. Some of the most impressive terraces are near the town of Banaue. The Ifugao call them the Stairway to Heaven, and many travelers consider the terraces one of the great wonders of the modern world. Tourists can trek the terraces at Banaue, some of which are still thriving rice operations.

CORREGIDOR This tiny island, which lies just west of Manila, was the scene of fierce fighting between Japanese and U.S. forces during World War II. Visitors can tour the ruins of barracks and explore tunnels that were used as a hospital for wounded U.S. soldiers and as a headquarters for military leaders. Travelers will see bullet holes and grenade burns everywhere, as well as items that soldiers left behind, some of which have never been moved. There is also a small museum that features uniforms and weapons, a Japanese cemetery, and a memorial to the thousands of soldiers who died there.

INTRAMUROS Built in Manila in the 1570s, the walled city of Intramuros is the former Spanish colonial capital. Plazas, well-planned streets, fifteen churches, six monasteries, and the Governor's Palace once existed within the walls. But bombings destroyed the city during World War II. San Augustin Church, the oldest stone church in the Philippines, is one of two structures that survived. The church's baroque architecture and murals draw many visitors. Tourists also stop at Casa Manila, a restored colonial-era house, and the prison and dungeon of Fort Santiago. The Rizal Shrine Museum, which honors national hero José Rizal, stands in Intramuros.

LAKE TAAL Many Filipinos and visitors travel to central Luzon to take in the views at Lake Taal, a sparkling body of water in the middle of a large crater. Taal volcano, a small mountain that lies in the center of the lake, attracts climbers. At the peak, the crater contains a lake with its own small island in the middle.

archipelago: a group of many islands scattered in a large body of water

Communist: someone who follows or believes in Communism, a political and economic model based on the idea of common rather than private property. In a Communist system, the government controls all goods and theoretically distributes them equally among citizens.

coral reef: an underwater limestone formation made up of the skeletons of marine animals called corals. A coral reef is a complex ecosystem that is home to a wide range of plant and animal species.

dialect: a variation of a language that is used by a certain group of speakers. A dialect can be characterized by pronunciation, grammar, or vocabulary.

government-in-exile: a temporary government that is moved to or formed in a foreign land by exiles who hope to rule when their country is liberated. Exiles leave their native countries voluntarily or are thrown out by force.

guerrilla: a member of a small combat group that works to destabilize a government or other authority. Guerrillas work to gain support for their cause from the general population while at the same time harassing and attacking their enemy, often through surprise raids or sabotage.

jeepney: a former military jeep or truck converted for public transportation and painted in a colorful design

martial law: an emergency form of government under military rule. Martial law is temporary and may be organized during a natural disaster, an economic crisis, political upheaval, a war, or other emergency situation. During martial law, military laws are substituted for civil laws.

monsoon: a seasonal wind that blows across southern Asia. From December to March, the monsoon blows cool, dry air from the northeast. It blows from the southwest from June through September, bringing heavy rains.

nationalism: a people's sense of belonging together as a nation, sharing feelings of loyalty to their country and pride in their culture and history

patron saint: a saint chosen to protect a country, place, group, profession, or event. Saints are holy people who are seen as heroes by their religions for their actions and dedication to their faiths.

al-Qaeda: a terrorist organization headed by Osama bin Laden that supports the activities of Muslim extremists throughout the world. The term *al-Qaeda* means "the base." Members of al-Qaeda believe the governments of Muslim countries that do not follow Islamic law should be overthrown. They also consider the United States and its allies the enemies of Islam.

Abinales, Patricio N., and Donna J. Amoroso. *State and Society in the Philippines*. Lanham, MD: Rowman & Littlefield Publishers, 2005.
This title explores the tensions that exist between the government and society in the Philippines, with a focus on government reform and economic development.

Balisacan, A. M., and Hal Hill, eds. *The Philippine Economy: Development, Policies, and Challenges*. New York: Oxford University Press, 2003.
This book, which focuses on economic trends since the 1980s, examines all major aspects of the Philippine economy and the country's development policy.

Broad, Robin. *Plundering Paradise: The Struggle for the Environment in the Philippines*. With John Cavanagh. Berkeley: University of California Press, 1993.
This look at the environmental politics of the Philippines addresses the destruction of the country's natural resources and how ordinary citizens are fighting to halt the plunder.

Cable News Network. *CNN.com International—Asia News*. 2005.
http://edition.cnn.com/ASIA/ (July 10, 2005).
This site provides current events and breaking news about the Philippines, as well as a searchable archive of past articles.

Canlas, Luzano P. *Philippines' 2 Millennium History*. Bryn Mawr, PA: Infinity Publishing, 2000.
This book offers a concise history of the Philippines.

Colin-Jones, Graham, and Yvonne Colin-Jones. *Philippines: Quick Guide to Culture and Etiquette*. Portland, OR: Graphic Arts Center Publishing, 2004.
This title discusses traveling in the Philippines, with a focus on daily life, culture, families, and celebrations.

Europa World Yearbook, 2004. Vol. 2. London: Europa Publications, 2004.
Covering the Philippines's recent history, economy, and government, this annual publication also provides a wealth of statistics on population, employment, trade, and more.

Karnow, Stanley. *In Our Image: America's Empire in the Philippines*. New York: Ballantine Books, 1990.
This book, by a journalist who covered Asia for thirty years, discusses the affect the United States and its policies has had on the Philippines, from its colonial period to present day.

Kirk, Donald. *Looted: The Philippines after the Bases*. New York: St. Martin's Press, 1998.
This book recounts what happened to U.S. military bases in the Philippines after the United States withdrew in the early 1990s.

Linn, Brian McAllister. *The Philippine War, 1899–1902.* **Lawrence: University Press of Kansas, 2002.**
This detailed account traces the events of the Philippine War.

Miller, Stuart. *Benevolent Assimilation: The American Conquest of the Philippines, 1899–1903.* **New Haven, CT: Yale University Press, 1982.**
This book tells the story of the Philippine War and looks at the Americans—presidents, senators, generals, and soldiers—who played key roles in the conflict.

"PRB 2004 World Population Data Sheet." *Population Reference Bureau (PRB).* **2004. http://www.prb.org (July 10, 2005).**
This annual compilation of statistics provides a wealth of data on the Philippines' population, birth and death rates, fertility rate, infant morality rate, and other useful demographic information.

Schirmer, Daniel B., and Stephen Rosskamm Shalom, eds. *The Philippines Reader: A History of Colonialism, Neocolonialism, Dictatorship, and Resistance.* **Boston: South End Press, 1987.**
Through documents and articles, this book examines the history of the Filipinos' struggle for independence and social justice.

Steinberg, David Joel. *The Philippines: A Singular and a Plural Place.* **Boulder, CO: Westview Press, 2000.**
This book offers insight into the diverse and complex culture, people, and politics of the Philippines.

Turner, Barry, ed. *The Statesman's Yearbook: The Politics, Cultures, and Economies of the World, 2004.* **New York: Macmillan Press, 2003.**
This resource provides concise information on the Philippine history, climate, government, economy, and culture, including relevant statistics.

BBC Country Profile: The Philippines
http://news.bbc.co.uk/1/hi/world/asia-pacific/country_profiles/1262783.stm
The BBC presents an overview of the Philippines.

Brainard, Cecilia Manguerra, ed. *Growing Up Filipino: Stories for Young Adults*. Santa Monica, CA: PALH, 2003.
In this collection of short stories, twenty-nine Filipino American writers address family, friendship, love, and home life in both the Philippines and the United States.

De la Cruz, Melissa. *Fresh Off the Boat*. New York: HarperCollins, 2005.
This novel relates the struggles a Filipina teenager faces as she adapts to a new life in the United States after immigrating with her family from Manila.

Economist.com. "Country Briefings: Philippines." *Economist.com*
http://www.economist.com/countries/Philippines/
This site provides recent news articles about the Philippines and a profile of the country.

Frank, Sarah. *Filipinos in America*. Minneapolis: Lerner Publications, 2005.
Enriched with historical quotes and primary source material, this book looks at the experience of Filipino immigrants in the United States.

Gelle, Gerry G. *Filipino Cuisine: Recipes from the Islands*. Santa Fe, NM: Red Crane Books, 1997.
This book provides an introduction to Filipino food and cooking.

Hertenstein, Jane. *Beyond Paradise*. New York: Morrow Junior Books, 1999.
Only a few months after fourteen-year-old Louise moves with her missionary parents from Ohio to the Philippines, Japan invades her new country. This is the story of how Louise becomes a prisoner of war in an internment camp during World War II.

INQ7.net
http://www.inq7.net/
This site offers up-to-the minutes news about the Philippines.

National Commission for Culture and the Arts
http://www.ncca.gov.ph/
This site features articles and information about culture and the arts in the Philippines.

The Official Government Portal of the Republic of the Philippines
http://www.gov.ph/
The official website of the Philippine government presents the latest government policies and information from all government departments.

Philippine National Statistical Coordination Board
http://www.nscb.gov.ph/
Covering everything from the people and the economy to the environment and the government, this site offers the latest Philippine statistics.

Further Reading and Websites

Philippines: Country Studies—Federal Research Division, Library of Congress
http://lcweb2.loc.gov/frd/cs/phtoc.html
This site provides an in-depth look at the history, people, economy, government, and politics of the Philippines.

Santacroce, John P. *Nine Thousand Miles to Adventure: The Story of an American Boy in the Philippines*. San Antonio: Four Oaks Publishing, 1998.
This adventure story tells what it was like to be an American teenager living on Clark Air Base from 1972 to 1975.

vgsbooks.com
http://www.vgsbooks.com
Visit vgsbooks.com, the home page of the Visual Geography Series®. You can get linked to all sorts of useful online information, including geographical, historical, demographic, cultural, and economic websites. The vgsbooks.com site is a great resource for late-breaking news and statistics.

Williams, Barbara. *World War II: Pacific*. Minneapolis: Lerner Publications Company, 2005.
This book presents a chronology of major battles fought in the Pacific region during World War II.

WOW Philippines
http://www.tourism.gov.ph/
The Philippine Department of Tourism's official website offers a wide range of information about the country.

Captions for photos appearing on cover and chapter openers:

Cover: The rice terraces of northern Luzon, built two thousand years ago, are often called the Eighth Wonder of the World.

pp. 4–5 Mount Mayon volcano, shown here at sunset, is one of the Philippines' most photographed sights. Until a 2001 eruption cracked the volcano's cone, it was the world's most perfectly symmetrical cone. Frequent eruptions mark Mayon as one of the most dangerous volcanoes in the world.

pp. 8–9 Skyscrapers line the horizon in the Makati business district of Manila, the capital of the Philippines. Consisting of seventeen different cities and municipalities, Metro Manila has a population of more than 10 million people.

pp. 20–21 A gate leads into the sixteenth-century walled city of Intramuros. Founded in 1571, the Spanish settlement was home to the Spanish ruling classes. It remained largely intact until World War II, when U.S. bombs destroyed it during the Battle of Manila. Most of the walls and gates have been carefully restored.

pp. 38–39 Crowds of people gather outside the Black Nazareth Basilica in Manila. Approximately 80 percent of Filipinos are Roman Catholic, giving the Philippines the highest number of Christians of any Asian country.

pp. 44–45 Costumed girls participate in the Sinulog parade on Cebu.

pp. 56–57 Filipinos dry and winnow rice in a field. Winnowing rice separates the chaff (outer hull) from the grain. The heavier grains fall onto trays, while the chaff is blown away by the wind.

Photo Acknowledgments
The images in this book are used with the permission of: © Rob Howard/CORBIS, pp. 4–5; XNR Productions, pp. 6, 11; © Steve Vidler/SuperStock, pp. 8–9; © John Elk III, pp. 10, 20–21; © Yann Arthus-Bertrand/CORBIS, p. 13; Courtesy Philippine Department of Tourism, Chicago, pp. 15, 17 (both); © Chris Stowers/Panos Pictures, p. 19; © Brown Brothers, p. 23; © Mark Downey/Lucid Images, pp. 24, 55; Dictionary of American Portraits, p. 27; Library of Congress, p. 28 (LC-USZC4-5958); © Grey Villet/Time Life Pictures/Getty Images, p. 30; Martin Luther King Jr. Library, p. 31; © Trip/Art Directors, p. 32; © Robert Nickelsberg/Time Life Pictures/Getty Images, p. 34; © PhotoDisc Royalty Free by Getty Images, p. 35; Office of the Press Secretary, Philippines, p. 36; © Peter Treanor/Art Directors, pp. 38–39, 46, 58 (top); © Christophe Loviny/CORBIS, p. 40; © Peter Barker/Panos Pictures, p. 43; © Paul A. Souders/CORBIS, pp. 44–45, 52; © ROMEO GACAD/ AFP/Getty Images, p. 47; © A. Tovy/Art Directors, p. 48; © John Pennock/Lonely Planet Images, p. 49; © Carl Mydans/Time Life Pictures/Getty Images, p. 51; © Romeo Ranoco/Reuters/CORBIS, p. 53; © Dave Saunders/Art Directors, pp. 56–57, 61; © Val Huselid/Independent Picture Service, p. 58 (bottom); © Cory Langley, p. 62; Courtesy International Geothermal Association, p. 63; Master Sgt. Val Gempis/Air Force News Agency/www.af.mil/news, p. 64; © Audrius Tomonis—www.banknotes.com, p. 68 (both); Laura Westlund, p. 69.

Front cover: © John Elk III. Back cover: NASA.